THE
ALCHEMICAL
TAROT

Rosemary Ellen Guiley
and
Robert Michael Place

Thorsons
An Imprint of HarperCollins*Publishers*

Thorsons
An Imprint of HarperCollins*Publishers*
77–85 Fulham Palace Road,
Hammersmith, London W6 8JB

1160 Battery Street,
San Francisco, California 94111–1213

Published by Thorsons 1995
3 5 7 9 10 8 6 4 2 1

© Rosemary Ellen Guiley
and Robert M. Place 1995

Rosemary Ellen Guiley and Robert M. Place
assert the moral right to be identified
as the authors of this work

A catalogue record for this book
is available from the British Library

ISBN 1 85538 301 2

Printed in Great Britain by
Woolnough Bookbinding Limited
Irthlingborough, Northamptonshire

THE
ALCHEMICAL
TAROT

Dedications

From Robert Michael Place
to my wife Rose Ann

and
From Rosemary Ellen Guiley
to my dear friend and alchemist
Joan Sckrabulis

CONTENTS

FOREWORD

At first glance, nothing might seem more unexpected than the great flowering of Tarot which has occurred in the last part of the twentieth century. Despite whatever doubts might arise as to the benefits of science and technology, no one really can question their hold on our world. How, then, can we account for the fascination with an esoteric system of images which appear hopelessly outdated, and which previously only interested small groups of occultists?

As Robert Place and Rosemary Ellen Guiley point out, the movement of science itself may point to an answer. The popular notion of science as wholly mechanistic is itself out of date, and has been for much of this century. Quantum physics, big band cosmology, relativity and Heisenberg's uncertainty principle all helped to disrupt the classic vision of the universe as a smooth-running clock, steadily ticking away, with humans somehow standing outside it to observe and analyse the machine. When we consider as well the effects of discoveries in mythology, archaeology, tribal and prehistoric art and metaphysics, and, within our own culture, depth psychology, we suddenly find ourselves in a world very different from the one we inherited from the 18th and 19th centuries. It begins to look as if that mechanistic world view is not really the dominant picture of the world at all, but is simply a temporary aberration.

If the observer takes part in creating the world, why not

take an active part? And if we wish actively to alter our lives, images work a great deal better than explanations, charts, sermons or even weekend workshops. The Tarot enables people deliberately to transform their lives because it works in pictures, not words. We can play with them, stare at them, use them in meditation, make up stories about them – and yes, lay them out in 'readings'. Most of the time, readings do not really tell the future, but they do tell us a lot about ourselves. And they also give us tools to start doing something with the information.

The Tarot works so well because the images are not random. They actually form a coherent step-by-step description of human development, from basic life issues all the way to the spiritual awakening variously described as 'enlightenment' or 'mysticism'. But this description is by no means limited to Tarot cards alone. We find it in Indian Tantra, in the Jewish mystical system called Kabbalah, in the mystery cults of the ancient world. And as The Alchemical Tarot so vividly demonstrates, this great story, the story told in the Tarot pictures, is very similar to the beliefs and practices of alchemy.

One of the many virtues of Place and Guiley's brief history of Tarot and alchemy is that it avoids making sweeping claims, particularly about the Tarot's origin. They do not say that the Tarot comes directly from alchemy, only that alchemy probably contributed to the ideas and images which went into the creation of the cards. And yet, when we look at alchemical prints and set them next to traditional Tarot images, the resemblances will often leap out at us. Indeed, Robert Place began his journey to the creation of The Alchemical Tarot when he looked at an alchemical print and recognized the same structure as the World card in the Tarot.

Among the vast numbers of decks published in the past 20 years we can find several based on alchemy. Robert

Place's deck stands out by the elegance and charm of his art. The pictures speak to us directly, yet with great subtlety. Place has taken a large number of alchemical images and unified them in his own style. We should realize, however, that these are authentic alchemical scenes. The fact that they also serve as traditional Tarot cards demonstrates more than anything else the connections between the two traditions.

The symbolic connections suggest that both Tarot and alchemy refer to a particular way of looking at the world. Place and Guiley suggest that the Tarot is 'related to the spiritual death and rebirth symbolism of alchemy'. This is certainly true in the details. We might add, however, that both systems belong to a much older tradition, or perhaps we should say a much older state of mind. This state is the identification of human existence with the cycles of the plant world, a process of growing, dying, rotting and growing again. When we watch this endlessly repeating cycle, year after year, it seems strange that human beings should live once, die and not spring up again with new life. The idea comes to us that maybe we are doing something wrong. What would happen, we wonder, if we could somehow die while alive – give up our attachments to everything rigid in our psyches and our bodies – let them rot and disappear? Might we find ourselves reborn?

As well as the example of the plant world, another strain goes into the development of esoteric traditions, and in particular alchemy. This is the violent transformations experienced by shamans, especially during the period of initiation. These transformations are often involuntary, coming in the form of severe hallucinations. In many places, the hallucinations themselves form the marker that the spirits have chosen that particular man or woman for a shamanic calling.

The initiation involves the breaking down of the body.

Typically, the shaman (or shaman-to-be) finds him or herself attacked by spirits. These spirits will chop up the shaman with knives or strip the skin off the body – or boil him or her in a cauldron, the very image found in alchemy. The spirits will then reconstruct the body, in particular the skeleton. Or they will replace it with a new one, composed of some purified substance, such as quartz crystal. The new body will contain the power to heal, to travel to the spirit world and to understand the actions of the spirits in our ordinary reality. The shaman also gains the power to tell the future, reminding us that Tarot readings have a much older lineage than carnival fortune-telling.

Place and Guiley point out that alchemy probably took some of its imagery from the story of Osiris, whose brother Set dismembers him, cutting him into 14 pieces. Isis, Osiris's sister and wife, reassembles Osiris, and the restored god now becomes the salvation of dead souls. The connection of alchemy to this all-important Egyptian myth is certainly vital. At the same time, the Egyptian tale itself may have derived from earlier strains of shamanic initiations. In fact, Osiris may combine shamanism with that identification with the plant world mentioned above. According to scholars of Egyptian religion, Osiris served as a god of vegetation in early Egypt, long before his depiction as lord and saviour of the dead.

We should never forget that the various images of death, dismemberment and rebirth are not simply intellectual constructions. Whether as shamans or alchemists, people have actually experienced these things. The lush images of The Alchemical Tarot can help us remember.

Rachel Pollack

INTRODUCTIONS

Robert M. Place

O N a summer night, in rural New Jersey, in 1982, I had a dream in which I was walking through a room when the phone rang. The phone was also part of the dream, but its ringing woke me into lucidity while I continued dreaming.

With a feeling of utter amazement – that someone could actually call me in a dream – I picked up the phone. On the other end an international operator informed me that she had a person-to-person call for me from a law firm in England. I accepted the call, and then a secretary from the firm came on the line. She told me that she was sending me my ancestral inheritance. She could not tell me what it was, but only that it would come from England, would be kept in a box, and is sometimes called 'the key'. She added that I would know it when I saw it. Then she ended the conversation with some precautions on its use and misuse.

I awoke that morning with a feeling of excitement and expectation. All through the week I eagerly anticipated receiving my inheritance. At the end of that week a friend came over with his new deck of Tarot cards. It was the deck designed in England in 1910 by Arthur Edward Waite and Pamela Colman Smith. Although I was not unfamiliar with this deck, I now saw it in a new light – I knew that this was my inheritance.

Within a few days another friend gave me a deck called

the Tarot of Marseilles. That was my first deck, but soon I went into Manhattan to buy the Waite–Smith cards.

I began experimenting with the cards. At first I resolved not to read any books on the Tarot. I wanted to communicate directly with the images, unhindered by preconceptions. I did remember being shown the Celtic Cross spread in college. So I decided to begin with that, combining it with Jungian techniques of dream interpretation.

The Tarot taught me a great deal directly, but eventually I realized that to unlock its secrets further I needed to gather more information. I began reading everything that I could find on the Tarot, Gnosticism, alchemy and related subjects. Every table in my studio was soon covered with stacks of books reaching towards the ceiling, and I filled a large hardbound notebook with charts, lists and notes – at the time this seemed odd because I was not a writer, and had no plan to become a writer.

By 1987 my reading had become noticeably excessive to my wife and friends. I intuitively knew that I was on to something, but I was unable to explain what it was. One afternoon I was sitting in the living room reading *The Rosarium Philosophorum*, a sixteenth-century alchemical text, when a commentator on the radio began talking about the Harmonic Convergence. I had been hearing about this for a few weeks, but thought of it as just another New Age curiosity. However, this time it was different; the commentator said that during this period of spiritual transformation sensitive individuals all over the Earth would be experiencing a flood of information on spiritual subjects. Finally, someone had an explanation for what was happening to me; this intensity was a product of the time. In some way the soul of the Earth demanded it.

Shortly after 16 August – the day of the Convergence – I was reading the *Picture Museum of Sorcery, Magic, & Alchemy* by Emile Grillot de Givry, when I became fascinated by an alchemical hieroglyph representing the philosopher's stone. The design depicted a heart in the centre of a cross with images of the four elements assigned to each corner (*see below*). In a flash I realized that the symbolism in the design was entirely interchangeable with that of the World card in the Tarot.

Lapis Philosophicus

The heart, of course, was meant to be a symbol of the soul, and that it was in the centre of the elements meant that it was the soul of the world, the alchemical Anima Mundi, the matter of the stone. I remembered that the pose of the figure on the World card is identical to the dancing figure that the Egyptians used as a hieroglyph for one aspect of the soul, and that the symbols of the four evangelists that surrounded it are equated to the elements. Certainly, the World card represented this same anima of the world. This realization was like a key opening a lock. I sat mesmerized as it became obvious that the Tarot trumps are alchemical, and that the series of trumps outlines the alchemical opus. This insight happened in seconds, but it began a seven-year journey that led me to design this Tarot deck and to write this book.

From the beginning this journey was marked by synchronistic events that brought information to me, and led me on the right path. Synchronicity underlies all of alchemy; it is the place where the physical world and the psychic world connect. Because it imparts a personal meaning to events it is often difficult to talk about. My dream of my inheritance is one example; I will try to give some others.

One evening while we were travelling, my wife and I made plans to meet a friend for dinner. Through an unusual series of mishaps we arrived at the restaurant late and missed our reservation; this led us to browse in a nearby bookshop while we waited for a table – if we had eaten dinner on time the store would have been closed afterwards, so we would not have gone there. In the shop I came across a book which would prove to be instrumental in leading me to a reprint of instructional documents originally intended for the members of the Golden Dawn. Because of my dream, and the resulting connection with the Waite–Smith cards, I had come to think of A. E. Waite and Pamela Colman Smith as my benefactors. I knew that both had been members of the Golden Dawn, and I felt that in some way their spirits had guided me to this book.

In the book I read about a meditation technique practised by the Golden Dawn, in which a picture is visualized as a door, and in which opening that door, and entering through it, guides one to an inner realm (*see Chapter 5*). This was like a second key. I realized that using this technique with the Tarot I could progress through each trump card and perform the alchemical opus directly on myself. I started that day.

Although I could not explain why, I began the opus with the Magician instead of the Fool – the card that seemed like a more logical choice. After that, conscious logic had less and less to do with the process, as I gradually allowed myself to be guided by unconscious wisdom. Sometimes I would perform the meditation on consecutive nights – one card after another – then a month might go by before I was called on again. At times I would find myself sitting up in bed before sunrise – I am usually a late riser – with that undeniable recognition that it was time for the next card.

The morning of the winter solstice in 1987 was one in which I found myself sitting up before sunrise. With a feeling of being guided, I left the secure warmth of my bed and entered the studio. There I sat on the floor with the Wheel of Fortune card in front of me. I was facing south – as I had for the last few cards – but this time I realized that I must face east instead. So, I turned towards the east wall, which was lined with casement windows reaching almost from the ceiling to the floor, and entered that inner door.

This time, however, the experience refused to be contained on an inner plane. My eyelids were filled with a golden glow from the rising sun, and I gradually opened my eyes.

Years before, when I moved into that house, I had placed two rosewood figures on the window sill that was now directly in front of me. They were carved in India, and represented a man and a woman standing stiff and totem-like, nude, with their hands to their sides. Each was 30 cm (1 ft) high and the figures were identical in every detail except for their sexual characteristics. Now they stood there facing me as the sun rose directly between them. I continued to watch as it rose to form the apex of an equilateral triangle with the nudes at its base. The configuration was identical to the Lovers card designed by Smith.

This experience had a profound effect on me. I had set those figures in place long before I was even involved in alchemy or the Tarot. How could I have known that they would mark the sunrise on this solstice and create an image of the Lovers? I was not usually even awake at sunrise.

The symbolism was obvious. It combined the Lovers,

which marked the first alchemical conjunction, with the Sun, which was clearly the greater conjunction – the *hieros gamos*, or sacred marriage. That it happened with the Wheel of Fortune showed that this card was an overview, and a powerful pivotal point in the procession of the trumps. But for me the experience was more; it was a literal marriage of psyche and matter. My inner world and outer world had merged; I had experienced the *hieros gamos*.

On the vernal equinox in 1988 I was standing in a natural foods store in Manhattan when I was astonished by the title of a magazine on the rack. It was called *Gnosis*, and I was surprised that information on Gnosticism could be so readily available. Urged by my wife and our friend I bought that copy, and then subscribed.

The following summer I was reading *Gnosis* when my inner voice told me to submit copies of my drawings for publication. I did so, and within a week the Editor called me. He needed an illustration to accompany an article on Sophia in issue 13, and my drawings arrived just in time. In November my drawing for the Star was published along with a one page article that I wrote for it.

A few weeks later I received a letter from Rosemary Ellen Guiley, an author who had seen my article in *Gnosis*. Rosemary was writing a book, called *The Mystical Tarot*, and asked me to submit drawings of my cards. She agreed to include Temperance and the Devil in her book, and after it was published I received several copies.

At this time I had been concentrating my research on the early history of the Tarot, and was not as familiar with its history after the eighteenth century. Rosemary's expertise was the perfect complement to mine. It was in her book that I read for the first time a quote from Court de Gebelin in which he recounted how his insight into the mystic origin of the Tarot emanated from a flash of inspiration upon seeing the World card. The similarity with my own experience made the hairs on my neck bristle.

Later in Rosemary's book I read about a quarrel between A. E. Waite and Pamela Colman Smith over the placement of the Fool card. Smith wanted it at the beginning of the trumps, but Waite insisted that it should be placed before the World card – a kabbalistic placement based on Levi (*see page 123*). I was inclined to agree with Smith, and it had puzzled me that I included the Fool in the latter position during my Opus meditation. This, more than anything, convinced me that Waite's spirit was guiding me in this endeavour and that he was the benefactor in my inheritance dream.

Rosemary and I recognized a kindred spirit in each other, and decided to collaborate on *The Alchemical Tarot*.

I wish to thank Kathy, who dreamed that it would happen before I did, and who encouraged me to start. I also want to thank my wife, Rose Ann, and numerous friends who were mysteriously there at the right time, with the right advice, and Rosemary, my *soror mystica*, for her expertise in pulling this project together.

Rosemary Ellen Guiley

My road to *The Alchemical Tarot* began with a dream.

I have great respect for dreams, for they are the bearers of important messages to us. They can reflect mundane concerns such as 'day residues', the bits and fragments of things that happen to us in waking life. Dreams can also reflect fears and fantasies, and the unresolved, repressed conflicts that boil beneath the surface of our lives. Most important, dreams speak to us in a cosmic language of the soul – a language of symbols, which, as students of alchemy, the mysteries and the Tarot well know, are more powerful than words.

Dreamland is an interface. It is the place where the mundane world meets the Unus Mundus, which is the undifferentiated oneness of the space-time continuum, the Monad, the cosmic consciousness – or God. The interface is where the Unus Mundus breaks through to our consciousness. Here, in dreams, we meet the gods, goddesses, spirits and archetypes that express the Unus Mundus. They are mirror pieces of ourselves as well.

The Ancients understood this interface. For example, the early Greeks and Romans believed that the soul travelled while the body was asleep. The soul would go to other-worldly realms, where it could encounter spirits who mediated between humans and the gods. Plato called this realm 'the between'. The experiences in dreams were considered to have the same validity as experiences obtained during waking life.

Angels come to us in our dreams. They give us information, inspiration or comfort. We may recognize them in dreams as angels, or as mysterious beings, or as people who seem somehow special or different.

Some 12 years ago I began to have alchemical dreams involving an angelic being I called Silver Lady. The experiences began with periodic dreams that were significantly different from my normal dreaming pattern. I usually dream in colour, but Silver Lady dreams were in black and white. The settings were always unearthly, alien landscapes. They were often bleak, like deserts or the moon. Sometimes, the setting was nothing but a black void. The desert-like nature of the landscapes is significant, for in dreams the desert is often a symbol of spiritual transformation. The void corresponds to the nigredo, the initial stage of alchemy in which the *prima materia* undergoes 'death' prior to its resurrection as the philosopher's stone. The void also can be likened to the womb of the Great Goddess. All of these elements symbolically point to spiritual rebirth – a new phase, a falling-away of the old, the coming of the new. And Silver Lady was my psychopomp, my spirit guide.

She appeared in my dreams as a tall woman dressed in flowing, glowing silver garments; hence my name for her. We communicated telepathically. She usually kept her face turned away from me. When I was finally able to look upon it, I saw that it had no human features, but was an oval swirl of iridescent colour, like mother-of-pearl. At the time I did not know that hidden and unusual faces are characteristic of encounters with angels and otherworldly spirits.

Silver Lady

This is also symbolic of the mysteries, or that which is hidden from us, and which we must find on our own.

The purpose of these alchemical dreams seemed to be instruction from Silver Lady, though when I awoke I could never remember the content. I could remember images, however. I was shown other worlds where realities were unlike earth. I was taken into space and shown how to make a path of light for myself, by projection of thought. Looking back, it seemed that I was being introduced to the multi-dimensional nature of consciousness, and to the tremendous creative power of thought.

The dreams with Silver Lady became more frequent. They were wonderful and adventuresome, and I missed them if a period of time went by without one. I assumed her to be an angel.

In late 1986 I began work on a book that took me into the areas of magic, Goddess consciousness and the mystery schools. I saw a connection between Silver Lady and Goddess. Goddess rules the moon, and silver is her colour and metal. Moon and Goddess rule the intuition, the deep unconscious, the forces of nature and the interconnectedness of all things. They rule creativity – the ability to create with thought. Goddess is sometimes referred to as 'The Lady'. I still regarded Silver Lady as an angel who represented the feminine side of God.

One night I had a prototypical 'encounter'. Encounters with otherworldly beings follow a pattern. They often take place in the middle of the night, especially around 3 a.m. The percipient is often paralyzed. There is telepathic communication, but, more important, the percipient feels infused, such as with information, enlightenment or energy. There may be paranormal phenomena, such as levitation or psychokinesis.

On this particular night I awoke at about 3 a.m. to find Silver Lady standing beside the bed. She looked solid, though she glowed with a shimmery silver light. Her arms were outstretched towards me but not touching me. A stream of energy poured through her hands, entering me at the third eye chakra and at the heart chakra.

I can only describe this energy as like a datastream coming into me at a tremendous speed. I felt as though I were being downloaded by a cosmic computer. Information or knowledge was pouring in so fast that I could not discern what it was. I felt physically strained to absorb it, like I would explode if too much came in. Yet, I was powerless to stop it. I was paralyzed flat on the bed. Strangely, I felt no fear.

The infusion seemed to last for a long time, though most likely it was for only a few moments. I reached a point where I truly felt I could no longer absorb it. The connection terminated and Silver Lady vanished. I felt disoriented. I arose and shut the bedroom window, which had been open, and returned to bed and fell immediately asleep.

Years later I can still feel the power of the experience. I did not tell anyone about it for a long time, out of fear of ridicule. My interpretation of the infusion – the bits and pieces of which I could not comprehend – was that it was a 'blueprint'. I surmised that it pertained to my writing. Indeed, from that point on, I seemed to be guided along a specific path that opened into other realities.

To my dismay Silver Lady made no more appearances in dreams, nor did she appear in night visits. It seemed as though the infusion was the culmination of her mission. She did not disappear, but receded to a background in my consciousness.

In the autumn of 1991 I was able to meet up again with Silver Lady, through Eddie Burks, a medium and healer. Not only is Eddie a wonderful medium, he is a deeply spiritual man whose very presence is healing. During a visit I asked him if he could contact the angel realm for me for research I was doing for a book. Eddie agreed, and it was a remarkable session. The description of it is in my book *Angels of Mercy*.

At the end of the session I was able to ask one question: 'Who is Silver Lady?'

Silver Lady herself gave the answer. 'You do not have quite an accurate picture of me,' she said. 'I am not an angel, but am of the angel realm and of the human realm. My function is to be intermediate between the angel kingdom and the human kingdom for the purpose of interpretation. Seek not to identify me more closely at this stage.' And she receded once again into the background of my awareness.

I was puzzled at her admonition not to pursue her identity. I did not understand then that I had to discover it for myself, and not just be told.

The next time I encountered Silver Lady it was two and a half years later, in a breakthrough of consciousness. I was at work on this book, deep into the research, and receiving numerous flashes of insight and inspiration on the alchemical nature of the Tarot. When I undertake a book there is a certain point of transformation, and an acceleration of creativity. I begin the work as a researcher, reading, pulling together information, organizing material – all heavily left-brain, intellectual kinds of work. When I feel sufficiently inspired I begin to write. In the early stages the writing goes in fits and starts. At some point there is a change in the nature of the work. The spirit of the book descends into me, and I become it. It will not let go of me until the work is done. The mundane world recedes and the creative world comes forward, absorbing me into a kaleidoscope of multi-dimensions and altered states of consciousness, which ebb and flow as I shift gears back and forth between writing and other tasks. I let go of as much as I can in the mundane world to focus the maximum energy on the creative effort.

This crossover point is different for every book, and its intensity varies for every book. There are lightweight projects and heavyweight projects. *The Alchemical Tarot* was a heavyweight.

One day I was immersed in numbers mysticism, synchronicity and the Unus Mundus, and the works of Carl Jung and Marie-Louise von Franz. The spirit of *The Alchemical Tarot* had been flirting for some time with the edges of my consciousness, and now I felt it fully arrive in a flood of energy. I wanted to assimilate the energy, so I left work and began to meditate. I like to use crystals when I meditate, and I keep a bowl of them handy. It is my habit to pick out two for every meditation, selecting the shapes and colours which feel right at the moment. I hold them to absorb their energies. Now, I selected two, lit a candle and closed my eyes.

I am often aware of presences in meditation, which I perceive on the inner plane as fields of light or energy. These are not to be confused with the shifting forms of light that happen naturally when you close your eyes. These presences identify themselves to me through the intuitive voice. This time, I perceived a different field of energy, which identified itself as the Angel of Alchemy. An appropriate being, I thought, to usher in this work. As I studied this presence, I suddenly realized that it was Silver Lady. And, I was seeing her true identity.

What happened next was a series of realizations that were sequential, yet they piled one on top of the other so fast that it felt like a nuclear explosion. I suddenly comprehended a great web of matters, vast and eternal, complex and simple, with layers upon layers of subtleties, each piece unique to itself yet inseparable from the rest.

Silver Lady is the alchemist's Luna, the Queen, the metal silver, the divine feminine principle. She is the Tarot's High Priestess, the guardian and gateway to the Beyond, the

Unus Mundus. She is Goddess, ruler of the rhythms of life, the unconscious, the mysteries. She is magic personified.

I saw the iridescence that comprises her face, and realized it to be the peacock's tail, the *cauda pavonis*. The peacock's tail is the stage in alchemy that is an eruption of a brilliant array of iridescent colours, like a peacock spreading its tail in a fan, and it signifies the flowering and blossoming of the Opus. It precedes the albedo, which is the whitening or purification. Jung observed that the peacock's tail heralds the success of the Work, the imminent achievement of the philosopher's stone.

All of these associations, these interlocking layers, made themselves known to me at once.

I floated, timeless, suspended in Silver Lady's revelation.

As the meditation ended, I reminded myself of the two crystals I had intuitively selected. In my left hand was moonstone, a symbol of Goddess, and in my right was lapis, a symbol of the philosopher's stone. Even the date was synchronistically significant: it was the 13th. Thirteen is a number of the Goddess, for there are 13 lunar cycles in a calendar year. In numbers mysticism, 13 adds up to four, the number of wholeness and completion, which also has great alchemical significance. Maria Prophetissa, the famous Jewish alchemist who lived about the time of the first century BC, conceived the alchemical axiom, 'Out of the One Comes Two, out of the Two comes Three, and from the Third comes One as the Fourth.' Essentially, it means that the number four relates back to one, the Monad, or the Unus Mundus. The entire experience was contained within a mandala of wholeness.

Silver Lady, then, had revealed herself as a cosmic alchemist. It was a complex picture, bound up in universal mysteries that transcended my own Self, but yet it was an integral part of my own spiritual alchemy at work. I saw that Silver Lady is myself as alchemist, and at the same time alchemist of the cosmos. She is the *prima materia*, the Opus and the Stone, all in one, simultaneously.

Silver Lady is the psychopomp who guides me to the *fenestra aeternitatis*, the 'window into eternity', the hole in the space-time continuum that gives the alchemist a glimpse of the Unus Mundus. In the Middle Ages the Virgin Mary – another aspect of the Goddess – was described as the 'window of enlightenment'. That, too, is Silver Lady. She is the guide to the window, the guardian of the window. She *is* the window, and what lies Beyond as well.

I see the blueprint much more clearly now. It is the Great Work. It exists on many levels of great subtleties, and though I comprehend the nature of it, the totality of it remains beyond my comprehension, ineffable. It is the Great Work of my own soul; it is the Great Work of many souls, of all things in creation, which are all One.

Is this the final word on Silver Lady? I think not. She is multi-faceted, and alchemist is but one of her roles. Shift the perspective and different facets of the silvery gem come into view. She reveals what is needed when it is needed.

Silver Lady is also a mirror. She reflects my own soul's beauty. But it is not just my beauty; it is collective, the beauty of all. The beauty is there for all to discover. And Silver Lady is there, in many guises, standing at the thresholds to many paths which all lead to the same place.

Your path awaits. Light it.

ABOUT THE DESIGN FOR THE BACK OF THE ALCHEMICAL TAROT CARDS

THE rose is the essential symbol of alchemy. It is highly complex, symbolizing perfection, the mysteries of life, the point of unity of life and the cosmos. Because of its basic five-petal structure, it is associated with the pentagram, a symbol of the human microcosm and the *quinta essentia* within.

The rose here is the unified rose of alchemy. It is neither red nor white – the colours of the masculine/feminine polarities of alchemy – but is pink, the colour that results from the perfect unification of the two. Its stem and leaves are green, which is the raw colour of its origin.

The rose is presented in a *vesica piscis*, also known as a mandorla, an upright oval often used in mystical art to surround a sacred figure. The *vesica piscis* is a symbol of the vulva, and denotes an opening or gateway into the mysteries of life (or higher consciousness) through the Mother Goddess. The design is derived from the Egyptian hieroglyph of the same shape, *ru*, which means 'doorway' and 'vulva'.

Beyond the boundary of the *vesica piscis* half of the card is chequered, showing the white of the albedo stage separating from the black of the initial alchemical stage, the nigredo. The other half is red, the colour of the fourth and final stage, the rubedo. Behind the rose is the yellow of the citrinitas, the stage that announces the final reddening.

Both parts of the design are framed in blue. Blue is another hermaphroditic colour, and the perfect symbol of the unconscious because it symbolizes both the celestial heights of sky and the unseen depths of the sea – above and below, masculine and feminine. In alchemy blue is a catalyst. Its addition makes white appear whiter, and black seems darker when it contains a gleam of blue.

1

ALCHEMY AND THE TAROT

BOTH alchemy and the Tarot are steeped in mysticism and mystery. Both present to the initiate systems of eternal, dreamlike, esoteric symbols that have the power to expand consciousness and connect the human soul to the Divine. In the Alchemical Tarot the power of both traditions is combined to offer the initiate a potent tool for personal growth.

In following the path of the Alchemical Tarot, we can transcend the world of matter and rise into the world of spirit. There, the boundaries of time and space fall away. The symbols yield their secrets and we can glimpse the past, present and future, and see things in new ways. The cards can help us with the affairs of the mundane world, and with pushing out further frontiers on the higher planes.

One need only look at the Tarot trumps, with their images of love, death and rebirth, to see that they are related to the spiritual death and rebirth symbolism of alchemy. In fact, alchemical content is imbedded deeply in the Tarot, even in the earliest decks. Yet the exact relationship between alchemy and the Tarot remains partially hidden, just as the depths of their symbols retain their secrets. How did alchemy come to infiuence the Tarot and to be integrated into card symbols?

History and Development of Alchemy

Alchemy is much older than the Tarot; it is more than 2,000 years old, compared to several hundred years for the Tarot.

The word 'alchemy' is derived from the Arabic word 'alkimia'. 'Al' is the definite article (the), which in Arabic is normally attached to the noun. 'Chemy' has two possible derivations. first, 'kmt' or 'chem' was the Ancient Egyptians' name for their land; it meant 'the black land' (meaning black or fertile earth in contrast to desert). In this case the Arabic name would mean 'the Egyptian Art'. The second possible derivation is from the Greek word 'chyma', which means to fuse or cast metal. Indeed, early metallurgy is the most likely origin of the mystical science of alchemy.

Alchemy has had a long and venerable history in India, where it is still taught today under the name 'ayurveda', and in China, where it became associated with Taoism. However, our focus here will be on the development of Western alchemy, especially as it pertains to the Tarot.

Ancient Egyptian Roots

Western alchemy emerged out of Egypt. Initially it dealt with the science of metals and was not viewed as a spiritual path. Egyptian religion evolved out of a shamanistic prehistoric past, and it developed a complex body of magic formulae that were the beginnings of what we would call geology, metallurgy and chemistry. Among these were the techniques for separating gold, silver, copper, lead, iron, and tin from ore, the making of such alloys as bronze by combining copper and tin (when bronze was discovered it must have seemed like a type of gold made from base metal), dyeing, brewing, gilding, perfume-making, chemical recipes, and magic rituals for the embalming of the dead.

Embalming rituals, designed to insure the rebirth of the deceased, were alchemical in nature. The body was dismembered, reassembled, then chemically preserved. It was placed in a coffin (vessel), which represented a Mother Goddess, such as Isis, who was often depicted encircling the dead with her winged arms; in this way the dead were returned to the womb. At the funeral wheat or barley was placed in the hands of the deceased, and watered so that it would sprout in harmony with the resurrection of the body.

This entire process was said to come from Isis, the goddess of magic. Mythology tells that she first performed the rite in order to resurrect her murdered and dismembered husband, Osiris. Afterwards they were reunited in sexual union, and Isis gave birth to Horus, the god of the sun.

When Alexander the Great conquered Egypt he brought Greek culture and philosophy into contact with Egyptian mystical religion and magic. It could be said that this mixture was the beginning of what we know as alchemy in the West. The earliest extant alchemical manuscripts are Egyptian papyri from Alexandria, the city founded by Alexander in 332 BC. They are texts on metallurgy, especially for making imitation metals for jewellery. These recipes call for adding small amounts of gold to other metals to make a product that appears to be all gold. The Leyden–Stockholm papyri, as these Alexandrian texts are called, also give formulae for bronzing metals, making purple dyes, culturing artificial pearls, and so on.

The Greek Philosophers

The syncretism that flourished in the Hellenistic era provided the seed for a spiritual focus on alchemy that attempted to explain it in terms of Greek philosophy. The Ancient Greek philosophers were intensely curious about the physical world and desired to discover what was lasting in a human being – that part of the individual that can transcend death. A philosopher was a scholar and a thinker, who studied nature and who sought to find truths about life and the universe. Today we would call such a person a scientist.

Plato and Aristotle, the towering giants of Greek philosophy, believed that the material world was composed of four elements, named earth, fire, air and water. These four elements also had four qualities: earth was cold and dry; fire was hot and dry; air was hot and moist; water was cold and moist. Furthermore, the elements were mutable: one could be changed into another through its shared quality. This mutability applied to minerals as well, which differed from metals in being composed of a 'smoky exhalation' (hot and dry), whereas metals were composed of a 'vaporous exhalation' (moist and cold). Everything also had a purpose, which was a striving towards its final and perfect state. Thus, it was believed that all metals eventually would mature into gold if left in the earth long enough.

Parallel to the material world was a spiritual one where the perfect essence or idea of all material reality existed. Plato called these spiritual essences 'archetypes'; he believed that everything on the material plane emanated from its spiritual archetype, and that all the archetypes emanated from one pure idea – the prime mover, or God. One could know this non-material world through the intellect by comprehending the structure and mathematical principles behind material objects. Plato felt that we do not learn these principles by abstracting them from sensual knowledge, but by an intuitive process that he called 're-remembering'. In other words, by acquiring knowledge of truth we reunite ourselves with our spiritual origin – the place where the knowledge resides.

Modern scholars regard Zosimos, a Greek who lived in Panopolis, Egypt, at the end of the Hellenistic period (the third century AD), as the oldest known 'authentic' alchemist. His works are known from an encyclopedia-like compendium of 28 alchemical texts, collected in the seventh and eighth centuries in Byzantium. These texts describe a labour, guided by dreams and visions, in which base metals were ennobled into gold by first 'killing' them and then 'resurrecting' them (a process similar to Egyptian embalming).

This transformation was meant to imitate the natural maturation process already mentioned, but the alchemist, with the aid of a catalyst, could produce the change more quickly than nature. His method depended on the production of a series of four colours – black, white, yellow and red – obtained through the materials 'divine', or sulphur water (divine and sulphur are the same word in Greek). To the early alchemists colour was the most important characteristic of metal, which is why it is possible that the creation of an alloy or a gilded surface could have been mistaken for a true transformation. Thus, it was natural that the alchemists would look for colour changes to mark the stages of their work. Zosimos named the magical catalyst that was necessary for the transformation as the powder *xērion*, which was translated into Arabic as 'aliksir', then into Latin as 'elixir', and finally became known as the philosopher's stone. Zosimos credits the source of his knowledge as Maria 'The Jewess', who may have been a Syrian alchemist from another and older school, although some scholars believe that she is totally mythical.

The developing mystical elements of alchemy together with the metallurgical recipes made for an exotic combination. For example, another early alchemical work, the *Codex Marcianus*, now in Venice, contains a translated text which asserts that it was written by Isis to her son Horus. In it she tells him the secret of making gold and silver, a secret she coerced from angels by withholding her sexual favours.

By the fourth century AD a coalescence of the philosophy

of Plato and mystical traditions from various parts of the Hellenistic world (including the mystery schools, Gnosticism, astrology, and others) produced a group of philosophers known as Neoplatonists. Prominent among these thinkers was the Greek philosopher, Plotinus (AD 205–270). Plotinus postulated that the Divine or the One is absolutely transcendent, completely beyond material duality, and of a nature completely incomprehensible to the human mind. The One could only be described through the use of negative statements – non-material, unlimited, etc. Although he is called Zeus or God, we can infer that he is neither masculine nor feminine. In creating the world the One had to manifest as a series of intermediaries, called emanations, in order to bridge the seemingly insurmountable chasm that existed between the One and the material plane.

Plotinus named the first emanation Nous, which means 'thought' or 'mind'. Just as we can create a thought which seems to have a life separate from our own, Plotinus reasoned that the One created Nous, then Nous created the Anima Mundi (the world soul, a concept that he borrowed from the Stoics), and the Anima Mundi in turn created the world. To achieve union with the One, the mystic could meditate on these emanations and in that state rise up through them back to their source. Later Neoplatonists, especially Iamblicus, added to the list of emanations, producing a complex hierarchy of planetary spirits, angels and demons.

The Medieval natural philosophers would call the divine One the Unus Mundus (world of the one), and recognize it as the initial unity from which all reality comes. In the sixteenth century, the alchemist Gerard Dorn would come to identify the Unus Mundus with the philosopher's stone. However, perhaps because of the womb-like nature of this conception, or maybe because of an unconscious need to balance a patriarchal society (as Jung suggests), alchemists from the fourth century on most strongly identified the One with its feminine emanation, the Anima Mundi.

The alchemists equated the Anima Mundi with what Aristotle had called the *prima materia* (first matter), an invisible substance that held the four elements together, and permeated all matter. Sometimes it was conceived of as a fifth element and therefore called *quinta essentia*. All these names eventually became synonymous, but whatever it was called, to release it from matter and create a transformative substance solely composed of this divine essence became the focus of the alchemical work. The alchemist came to view the evolution of base metal into gold as a Neoplatonic ladder of ascent, as important as the planetary emanations, and leading to the Anima Mundi.

Alchemy and the Arabic World

The Arabian army, under Amribn al-Ass, conquered Egypt by AD 642, bringing Arabs into contact for the first time with a large group of working alchemists. By the eighth century the Nestorians, who originated in Byzantium, would form another avenue for alchemical knowledge to enter the Arabic world. In the fifth century they had broken from the Orthodox Church and emigrated east, where they taught Hellenistic philosophy and translated Greek texts, including alchemical ones, into their language (Syriac). By the eighth and ninth centuries, Syriac texts were translated into Arabic. Additionally, during this period the Islamic Empire under the Umayyad rulers spread east to the Indus River, where there was ample opportunity to share influences with Indian alchemists. Wherever they encountered it, Arabs were quick to learn the philosophical science. In fact, the great alchemists from this period are Arabic.

The eighth-century Arabian alchemist Jabir ibn Hayyan, known in medieval Europe as Geger, was a member of the mystical Islamic movement known as Sufism. Sufis incorporated many Neoplatonic tenets into their Islamic asceticism. Like all mystics they strove for a personal experience of the divine, so it was natural that Jabir would be attracted to alchemy. Jabir developed a theory which became common to all subsequent alchemical texts. He said that all metals seemed to contain a balance of the four qualities; that is, they are cold and dry externally, and hot and moist internally. This was due to the fact that they were formed in the earth by the union of a substance that he called sulphur or 'earthy smoke' with another which he called mercury or 'moist vapour'. Sulphur and mercury became a masculine and feminine polarity in alchemy, similar to yang and yin in Taoist philosophy.

Although Jabir's references to mercury and sulphur are symbolic, the discovery of the actual liquid metal, mercury, *circa* 300 BC, coincides with the beginning of alchemy and seems to be crucial to its development in both the East and West. The original process of gold plating involved dissolving gold in mercury to form an amalgam, which was painted on the heated base metal. Heat was then increased until the mercury vaporized, leaving the gold on the surface. Scholars believe that some early alchemical texts actually describe the production of imitation gold that could be made in this way or by making a type of paint which mixes gold with sulphur.

Jabir also infused a great deal of mystical number symbolism into alchemy. He attached great importance to the numbers 1, 3, 5 and 8, and to their total, 17; for instance, he wrote that metals have 17 powers. It is most likely that these numbers are derived from Neoplatonic magic squares, which were squares composed of nine equal boxes containing numbers that, whether added diagonally or orthogonally, always equalled the same sum.

Al-Razi, a ninth-century Arabic alchemist, introduced the

necessity of accurate weights and measures, and recorded in detail his laboratory apparatus, much of which is still used by modern chemists. The Arabs were the perfecters, if not the inventors, of distillation. Parallel to their technical contributions, in the tenth century, Mohammed ibn Umail (known in Latin as Senior) added much to the mystical side of alchemy in his many writings, the most famous of which is the *Turba Philosophorum* (convention of philosophers), which describes a debate between Hermes, Socrates, Aristotle and other philosophers.

European Mystical Philosophy

Alchemy was not known in mainstream Europe until the twelfth century. Among the first westerners to be acquainted with alchemy were the Knights Templar, who during the Crusades had adopted the teachings of the Druses, a myst-ical pagan sect within the Islamic world. In the eleventh and twelfth centuries, the Islamic empire in Spain lost territory to Christian rulers. With the help of Jews, who were able to act as intermediaries between the two cultures, Spain became a mixing pot for the two cultures.

Jewish and Islamic scholars were invited to the court of Frederick II in Sicily, and the Knights of St John opened communication with the East on the island of Rhodes. Due to this influx of different peoples, Sicily, Spain and southern France rapidly became multicultural communities. In these areas Jewish and other scholars began to translate Arabic and Greek texts into Latin, which made them available to the rest of Europe. The first of these texts was the *Book of the Composition of Alchemy*, translated into Latin by the Englishman Robert of Chester in 1144. By the thirteenth and fourteenth centuries the art of gold-making was integrated into Western mystical philosophy.

European alchemists traced the origin of their craft to the

mythic Egyptian author, Hermes Trismegistus ('thrice great Hermes'). The *Hermetica*, which are the texts ascribed to him, were actually written in Greek and Latin by Neoplatonic Greek and Egyptian philosophers living in Roman Egypt and using a common pseudonym. These philosophers accepted as fact that Pythagoras and Plato had studied with the Egyptian priests, who had secret knowledge passed on to them in a collection of books written by the god Thoth (who the Greeks equated with Hermes). The Egyptian books themselves, like the *Book of the Dead*, were written in hieroglyphics decipherable only to the priests. The philosophers could only imagine their contents, and did not question the assumption that they were the basis of their Greek tradition.

The alchemical process came to be called the *magnum opus* or the great work. The opus was the search for the elusive, transformative substance contained in all matter. This substance was, as we noted earlier, called by various names, such as the Anima Mundi, the *quinta essentia*, the Unus Mundus, or the philosopher's stone (also called the *lapis philosophorum*, or *lapis*). To find it, alchemists had to determine the correct chemical procedure – a lengthy and difficult process of trial and error, with obscure symbolic texts as their only guide. (In fact, the word 'gibberish' was originally a description of the writings of Jabir, derived from his Latin name, Giber). The vivid, symbolic and allegorical nature of alchemy is due to the fact that alchemists relied on dreams, visions and revelation in their work. Since no two alchemists experienced exactly the same dreams and visions, alchemical texts tend to be vague and even contradictory.

The philosopher's stone was believed to have the power to transform base metal into gold. Taken as a medicine, it was a panacea. Some even believed that it was an elixir of life that could bestow immortality. Paralleling this chemical transformation was a spiritual transformation of the alchemist himself that was as necessary to the process as any physical component. When the *lapis* was found the alchemist was said to simultaneously achieve spiritual perfection (*gnosis*) making a mystical connection between him and the subject of his work.

In 1357 a French scribe and book dealer, Nicholas Flamel, bought a rare, old gilded book, *The Book of Abraham the Jew*, filled with strange illustrations and instructions for the transformation of metals into gold. With the help of his wife, Perrenelle, he began the difficult and lengthy process of carrying out the almost incomprehensible instructions. By Flamel's own account, they struggled for 25 years, day and night, before they were successful. It was the surreal illustrations, gathered in the centre of the book, and not accompanied by any written explanation, that held the secret of the opus. Flamel carefully copied them, and showed his copies to anyone who came into his bookshop, but this was of no help. In the end he took the drawings to Spain, where by luck or grace he met an old Jewish scholar who helped him decipher them.

After their success the couple used their sudden wealth to endow 14 hospitals, three chapels and seven churches in Paris, and others in Boulogne. They also helped the poor. In their will they left numerous houses as well as money for the benefit of the homeless. According to legend, having also discovered the secret of immortality, the Flamels only faked their deaths and moved to India with enough gold to last many lifetimes. They were reported to have been seen at the Paris Opera in 1761, and there are other accounts of their appearing throughout the centuries.

Flamel's account, and other equally fantastic stories, helped to popularize alchemy in Europe (in fact, after the Flamels' death their property was so thoroughly searched for pieces of the philosopher's stone that their house was reduced to rubble). Despite its fanciful quality, the ideas in alchemy were in strict accord with the best philosophical and scientific thinking of their time. Many of the most brilliant minds in the late medieval and Renaissance periods were those of alchemists, including Arnald of Villanova (1240–1313), Roger Bacon (1214–94), Albertus Magnus (1193–1280), and Paracelsus (1493–1531). Even men such as Robert Boyle (1627–91), who was critical of alchemists and helped lay the foundations of modern chemistry, believed he had achieved alchemical transformations in his work. The philosopher René Descartes (1596–1650) was interested in alchemy, as was Isaac Newton (1642–1727), who discovered the law of gravitation.

Newton devoted a large percentage of his study to alchemy and philosophy, but because of the unreceptive scientific climate during his life he never published his alchemical treatises. However, his theory of gravity is based on the concept of an invisible force existing between bodies – an idea which is common to Hermetic philosophy. In addition he used the alchemical term 'attraction' (which suggests an animate world) to describe it. Throughout his life he considered science a form of worship or a mystical quest.

The Importance of Symbols

As can be seen in Flamel's story, dream-like symbolic illustrations are an indispensable part of European alchemical texts. This development can be traced to the art of memory which was developed in Ancient Greece. In the classical world the memory arts were an essential part of the study of rhetoric, providing the discipline that helped one remember the points in a speech, or retain facts for a debate. The memory arts remained integral to formal education until the Renaissance, when the invention of the printing press made books more available to students.

Because pictures are more easily retained by the mind, and can incorporate many ideas simultaneously, the ancient texts recommended that the student create memory images which could be associated with each subject. It was specified that these images should be striking and dramatic. They could be unusual, vividly coloured, ugly, frightening, or extremely beautiful. Students were instructed to develop memory images of their own that could be easily associated with the facts of their subject. As can be demonstrated by the modern psychological technique called 'active imagination' (a Jungian therapy which employs the conscious visualization of, and interaction with, images from the unconscious), this imaging could easily evolve into a type of meditation that not only helped one retain information, but could heal the psyche. Over time it was natural that this art became associated with magic and mysticism.

Throughout the Middle Ages strange images called *notae* were commonly used by magicians. *Notae* were vivid images, usually based on astrological symbols, which the magician visualized while reciting incantations. and which aided him in invoking archetypal powers.

Medieval and Renaissance mystics also enlisted the aid of the memory arts in their quest for union with God. Most European mystical traditions can be traced to Neoplatonic philosophy. As we have seen, all Neoplatonic systems outline a series of emanations (such as a ladder) used by the One to descend to create the material plane. For example, the Jewish teachings called the Kabbala outline a version of these emanations in the Tree of Life, a meditative design that depicts 10 descending spheres called 'sephirot'. The design is likened to a descending tree whose roots are in heaven. The mystic at first visualizes vivid images for each emanation, and then visualizes the entire structure in order to ascend back up the ladder to reunite with the creator (Plato called the attainment of knowledge of the spiritual plane re-remembering). This technique was particularly developed by the Spanish mystic, Ramon Lull (b. 1232), who was the first Christian Kabbalist, and later by Giordano Bruno (b. 1528), a Dominican friar who was expelled from his order because of his ideas.

Memory images originally were intended to be personal and kept solely in the mind. In the Renaissance, however, these vivid images were captured in enigmatic illustrations, designed as aids in teaching. By 1400 woodblock prints (previously only used for textile designs) were being used to reproduce pictures on cards and in books, an advance that helped to popularize these visual aids. Thus, in 1422 the climate was right for the sensation created by a book called the *Hieroglyphica*, which arrived in Florence. Allegedly a Greek translation of an Egyptian work that explained the meaning of Egyptian hieroglyphics, in fact it only passed on a Greek misconception. Because the Ancient Greeks were unable to read hieroglyphics, they had assumed that hieroglyphics formed a type of allegorical picture incorporating many aspects of a subject into one image, and inviting the viewer's interpretation (or projection). In other words, hieroglyphics were thought to be a type of memory image.

The *Hieroglyphica* was translated into Latin, French, German and Italian, and became known throughout Europe. It was a major infiuence in developing the Renaissance trend for symbolic engravings called 'emblems' or 'hieroglyphs', created by prominent artists – including Albrecht Dürer – and used to encapsulate various fields of knowledge, especially alchemy.

By the seventeenth century, interest in alchemy had reached a peak, and an unprecedented quantity of enigmatically illustrated alchemical books were published – including the many works of Michael Maier, Jacob Böhme, and even a book with pictures and no written text, the *Mutus Liber* ('Silent Book').

Paracelsus, one of the greatest alchemists and the founder of modern medicine, defined alchemy as the transformation of one natural substance into another – one fit for a new use. He created non-herbal medicines, which he considered the main physical goal of alchemy. However, he believed equally that the true quest of the alchemist was his own spiritual transformation. The students of Paracelsus tended to progress in one of two directions: those who developed the science of medication, which led to modern medicine and then chemistry; and those who abandoned the laboratory to search for spiritual gold within, a course which led to mystical philosophies like Rosicrucianism.

The spiritual quest had been part of alchemy since ancient times, but from the time of Paracelsus it increasingly became the primary objective of alchemy. These alchemists wanted to separate themselves from those who were interested in alchemy only as a means to wealth. Alchemists who were solely materialistic were called 'puffers' because of their impatient use of the bellows to keep the fire hot and speed up the process (most alchemical texts recommended slow heating at a moderate temperature).

Others sought riches and fame through fraudulent claims of successfully transforming base metal into gold, which they accomplished by trickery. These charlatans caused alchemy to fall into disrepute. Fraud, and the discrediting of alchemy's underlying theories by scientific discoveries – for example, the components of water and air – influenced a growing view of alchemy as a pseudoscience. It received the death blow from Antoine Lavoisier in the eighteenth century, when he discovered that air contained an irreducible component which he labelled 'oxygine'. Lavoisier changed the definition of the term 'element' to mean one of these irreducible components instead of the classical four of air, earth, fire and water, and went on to develop modern chemical terminology. In 1808 the chemist John Dalton wrote that for each element there is a different unit of matter, called an 'atom', which is indivisible (he derived the word 'atom' from the Greek term for indivisible). Although these men contributed greatly to our body of scientific knowledge, by the end of the nineteenth century scientists would prove their assumption about the fundamental nature of reality to be wrong.

In the nineteenth century the symbolic, spiritual alchemical quest was revived, along with interest in the occult. This led to the formation of such groups as the Hermetic Order of the Golden Dawn, and, in the early twentieth century, the Ordo Templis Orientis (Order of the Templars of the East).

Jung and Modern Science

In the 1920s and 1930s the insights of Carl G. Jung, the great Swiss psychoanalyst and father of depth psychology, and his associates, made alchemy a respected area of psychological study. The alchemical process of transformation was found to be identical to the psychological process he called 'individuation'; he also saw that the alchemist's identification with the transformation of his subject was what Jung eventually termed 'synchronicity'.

Individuation can be described as the goal of the psyche itself, an ascent to the state of wholeness (Unus Mundus) to which the archetypal structure of the psyche leads. To Jung it is the psychological reality synonymous with the goal of mystical philosophies and religions. In the dreams of men an alluring female figure often guides the dreamer on this quest. Jung called her the 'anima', and she can be compared to the Anima Mundi. Parallel to the anima is the 'animus', a male personification of the unconscious often found in the dreams of women. The animus can be compared to the *anthropos* frequently visualized by alchemists as the god

Hermes (who was thought of as a male manifestation of the Anima Mundi). Alchemical texts commonly depict images of hermaphrodites to symbolize union of the masculine and feminine principles – a state of balance which can also be equated with individuation.

Synchronicity is defined by Jung as meaningful coincidences between internal psychic reality and external material reality. When an individual experiences synchronicity, an archetype has been activated. In Jungian terms the alchemist, through a process of synchronicity with chemical experiments, was led to a state of psychic wholeness in which his ego consciousness was integrated with his total psychic 'self', sometimes called the Higher Self. The self contains the entire psyche, the conscious and the unconscious. At its deepest level the unconscious is found to be vast and indistinguishable from the unconscious of others, a quality that Jung labelled the 'collective unconscious'. This, too, can be equated with the Unus Mundus, or the Anima Mundi.

One other frequently used Jungian term that will be useful to define is the 'archetype', a term that Jung borrowed from Plato. Jung realized that just as the human body has an anatomy common to all people, despite their superficial racial differences, the human psyche also has an anatomy – one that is collective and transcends cultural differences. And, just as the human body has a long evolutionary history that can be seen in its structure, Jung perceived that the psyche also carries its history in the form of primordial images, which he labelled the 'archetypes'. The anima and the animus are two examples of archetypes; there are countless others. They can be seen in the mythology, art and literature of all cultures. They transcend time and place, and on a personal level their appearance is always emotionally engaging, or numinous.

It is of interest to note that Jung's enchantment with

alchemy began in his own dreams. Between 1926 and 1928 he had a series of dreams in which he saw a previously unnoticed house annexed to his own. In each dream he wondered how he could not have known about the existence of this annex when it had apparently always been there. Finally, he dreamed he entered the annex and found that it contained a wonderful library, full of large sixteenth- and seventeenth-century books, hand-bound with pigskin, and illustrated with strange, symbolic copper engravings.

Jung interpreted his own house as a symbol of his consciousness. He realized that the annex represented something that belonged to him, but of which he was just now becoming conscious. He later learned that the library represented alchemy, a subject about which he was ignorant at the time, but which he soon began to study. Within 15 years he had assembled a library similar to the one in his dream.

With this treasure of symbols he was now able to understand certain dream motifs, which had previously puzzled him. His student, Marie-Louise von Franz, recalls an example in which one of Jung's patients had a dream of an eagle flying into the sky. In this dream the eagle began to eat its own wings, then dropped back to earth. Jung was able to interpret the dream, on a personal level, as a reversal of a psychic situation. Upon discovering an engraving of an eagle eating his own wings in the alchemical text *Ripley Scroll*, he was able to see that the image was also archetypal.

Jung saw that the experiences recorded by the alchemists coincided with his own experiences in analytical psychology, and that they gave him the necessary history of these experiences which he was looking for. More importantly, they taught him that the unconscious can be seen as a 'process'. It was through alchemy that Jung saw that the psyche is transformed or developed by the interrelationship between the conscious (ego) and the unconscious mind.

Concurrent with the findings of Jung, scientists studying physical reality could conceivably be said to have returned to alchemy when they found that the atom was not the smallest unit of matter. The first break came in 1897 when electrons were identified as small, negatively charged pieces of the atom. In 1911 the English scientist Ernest Rutherford discovered the nucleus, and went on to discover that it was composed of positively charged protons and neutrons with no charge. Rutherford found that the number of protons in the nucleus of a stable atom was always equal to the number of electrons in the shell (a balance of forces similar to Jabir's theory of the internal and external balance of sulphur and mercury in metals), and that the number of protons in an atom would determine which of the 106 elements it was to be.

In 1919 Rutherford completed the alchemical parallel when he transmuted the element nitrogen into oxygen by changing the number of its protons through the use of high energy radioactivity. In 1941 physicists Bainbridge and Anderson completed the first part of the alchemical quest when they bombarded mercury with neutrons, and thereby transformed it into gold.

The kinship to alchemy is even more startling as we proceed to the discoveries of modern quantum physics. Since the 1950s scientists have discovered more than 200 smaller particles within the atom. Rather than again redefining the term 'element', they chose to call them 'elementary' particles. The elementary particles inside the nucleus are called 'hadrons' from the Greek root for 'strong', and the ones outside the nucleus are called 'leptons', from the Greek root for 'weak' (they could have been easily named sulphur and mercury instead). All hadrons are made of six different, even smaller, particles called 'quarks'; they are named Up, Down, Strange, Charmed, Top and Bottom (at Harvard University, Top and Bottom are called Truth and Beauty).

There are also six different types of leptons outside the nucleus, creating a symmetry that underlies all matter.

Scientists now know that the atom, which was once thought of as a solid particle and the smallest building block of matter, is in reality mostly space with tiny elementary particles travelling through it. When scientists tried to determine whether these hadrons and leptons were really particles (therefore matter), or if they were waves (therefore energy), they made an even more startling discovery. In an experiment to determine if they were particles, they were found to be particles. But in an experiment to determine if they were waves, they were also found to be waves. Like the alchemists, modern researchers can no longer separate themselves from their work – they have found that their experiments respond to their expectations.

The basic components of matter are not solid at all. All matter is made of an elusive non-stuff that can appear as matter or energy; scientists cannot even say where a particle or wave is in space at any given moment. The entire sensual world is made of this non-stuff organized into numerical patterns of information that we can consider as the thoughts of the universe. This is where physics and psychology meet. Science has come full circle and has rediscovered the Anima Mundi.

The Emergence of the Tarot

Along with books on philosophy, mathematics and alchemy, the Islamic world probably introduced the game of cards to western Europe. It is known that early decks of playing cards existed in Islamic countries and in Turkey there are decks preserved from the fifteenth century that consist of four suits: scimitars, polo sticks, cups and coins. Most scholars agree that these cards stem from an older tradition, and because of their similarity to the earliest Western cards – with their suits of swords, staffs, cups and coins – they are the most likely source of inspiration for Western cards.

The first evidence of a card game in Christian Europe is a decree that banned the game in Florence in 1376. Before this time mention of cards is conspicuously absent from any lists of games, but after this date the evidence (about half of it negative, like the Florentine ban) shows that cards quickly spread through Italy, France, Spain, Switzerland, Belgium and Germany. Their rise in popularity at this time can be accounted for by the achievement of wood block prints on paper, an advance that made them more readily available.

The cards were called naibbe, nahipi, nabi or napis (names that are possibly derived from Arabic), and they mostly consisted of decks of 52 or 56 cards divided into four suits, much like a modern deck of playing cards. In each suit there were 10 pip cards, which simply depicted repetitions of the suit symbol corresponding to its number, and two or three court cards, which in their most complete form pictured a jack, a knight and a king. These were clearly not Tarot decks.

The first Tarot deck was created in northern Italy when an unknown designer added a fifth suit, containing 22 allegorical figures, to the already existing deck of cards (a queen was also added to the court cards). Like many aspects of popular culture we cannot give the exact time and location for its creation. However, we can narrow the time to around 1440. The first written record of the Tarot is from the court records in Ferrara, in 1442, and the oldest existing Tarot cards are a deck hand-painted – with gold-leaf backgrounds – by Bonifacio Bembo for the Duke of Milan, Francesco Sforza, *circa* 1445. According to historian Michael Dummett, the place of manufacture is most likely to be Milan, Ferrara or Bologna. These cities were all centres for the manufacturing of cards, and can display the earliest documentary evidence of their existence.

From the beginning the main purpose of the deck was for playing a card game in which the cards in the fifth suit acted as trumps for taking tricks, as in its English descendant, the game of bridge. In fact, the English word 'trump' is derived from the original Italian name for this suit, *trionfi*, which means 'triumph' (the entire deck was called *carte da trionfi*). Each of the trumps was clearly meant to be more powerful than the one before it (to triumph over it), so their order was standardized from their conception. Because printed playing cards were disposable (they were discarded when they wore out, or at times sacrificed in a bonfire at the end of Carnival) pre-eighteenth century cards are extremely rare, and many of them are unnumbered. However, we have enough evidence from surviving cards and written records to know that each major city where cards were played developed its own order.

The oldest reference to the use of cards for divination is a book published in Ulm in 1487, called *Mainzer Kartenlosbuch* (Mainz Fortunetelling Book). It lists divinatory meanings for each card in a standard 56 card deck. *Le Sorti*, a book published in Venice in 1540, describes a method of divination using only the king, knight, jack and six other cards from the suit of coins. Although these books do not necessarily refer to the Tarot, they prove that cards were used for divination at an early date. We can assume that other methods also existed, possibly using the Tarot (Merlini Cocai's sonnets written in 1527 provide divinatory associations for the trump images), and because so many pips were used in these systems, that divination at that time was influenced by number symbolism.

At the beginning of the sixteenth century the French invaded and occupied Milan, where they came in contact with this card deck, by then renamed the *tarocchi*. It is most likely that the French brought the *tarocchi* to their home country at that time. The Swiss were also politically involved in northern Italy in that period, and, like the French, may have taken the cards home. France, however, became a major manufacturer of the cards, and eventually shortened the name to *tarot*, first spelled *tarau* (in German the cards are called *tarock*).

The earliest evidence of the Tarot in France is a reference to the manufacture of the cards in Lyons in 1507. Later, Marseilles became the main manufacturing centre, and the order of the Marseilles trumps – which is closer to the Milan order than it is to any other Italian deck – came to be thought of as standard outside of Italy.

The Tarot cards seem to have emerged out of the philosophical ferment of the Renaissance, particularly the Italian Renaissance. The power of the Papacy was weakened at this time, and the residents of the prosperous, newly independent city-states were experiencing an atmosphere of intellectual freedom. They were guided by an overwhelming desire to reclaim classical art, culture and learning. Among the first Ancient texts to be made available to them were the Hermetica, works by Plotinus, and works on alchemy, magic and astrology. As a result, their culture was permeated with mysticism, along with a belief in freedom and human progress.

As mentioned earlier, the desire for knowledge and the heightened appreciation for the visual arts led to the creation of enigmatic images which were meant to fix the knowledge of arts and sciences in the memory. Medieval theologian Thomas Aquinas (1225–74) advocated the art of memory (Ars Memoria) as a devotional path, in which contemplation and meditation upon images could connect one to God. Scholars and magicians used Ars Memoria as a way of awakening the imagination. Images contained within them information that could be recalled and activated by visualizing the image, and power could be projected into higher realms of consciousness by manipulating the images. Some medieval scholars and magicians used astrological symbols (Ars Notoria) in rituals to contact presences in other planes.

The meditation upon symbols as a magical path reached its zenith in the work of Giordano Bruno (1548–1600), the ex-Dominican friar. According to Bruno, images could be charged with emotion and will. When organized to represent the divine order of the cosmos, they could enable the magus to participate in divine power itself. Cosmic consciousness – union with the Anima Mundi – could be obtained by holding all the images in the mind simultaneously. This was the driving passion behind the Renaissance need to acquire knowledge in all disciplines.

This mystical pursuit led to Renaissance artists creating works that organized the arts, sciences, virtues, etc. into encyclopedia-like sequences that simultaneously formed emanations on a Neoplatonic ladder of ascent. The most famous examples are Dante's *Divine Comedy* (Joseph Campbell has written a comparison of the Tarot to Dante's work), and Giotto's frescoes for the Arena Chapel in Padua (historian Ronald Decker has compared these to the Tarot designs). One of the best examples is the so-called Tarocchi of Mantegna, which is not a *tarocchi* but a series of prints, and is not likely to have been engraved by Mantegna. It consists of 50 images which organize the conditions of man, the arts, the sciences, the virtues and cosmology. It starts with the beggar and ends with the first cause (the creator). Many of the Mantegna images correlate with traditional Tarot symbols.

There are numerous other examples of these allegorical processions: prints, poems and a design for a seven-tiered theatre with allegorical statues. There was even an allegorical parade called the Trionfi, which was performed during Carnival (a pre-Lenten Christian festival popular throughout Italy). Gertrude Moakley, author of *The Tarot Cards*, theorized that this, combined with Petrarch's poem 'I, Trionfi', is the primary inspiration for the Tarot. Moakley equates the Tarot trumps to processional floats which portrayed an allegorical figure or virtue. While some of the correspondences fit nicely, there are enough gaps and missing links to question *trionfi* as the sole influence on the Tarot. It is most likely that the Tarot was not taken from any one source, but is simply another example of this trend in popular art at the time.

In creating this unique set of triumphal pictures, the designer, like any other artist, drew on many sources of inspiration. It is highly probable that alchemy, the prevalent science of the time, was one of them.

The majority of the fifteenth-century cards that have survived are hand-painted. This is most likely because they were unique, costly works of art which were highly valued. They were made for the noble patrons who could afford them, so by their very nature they are not part of the common tradition. In their time these cards were only seen by a few people. The Tarot cards that were available to most people, and which had more influence on future cards, were the printed ones. Therefore, the few prints that still exist are more important for discerning the nature of the tradition.

Although the original order of the cards varies, the cards that display the widest variation are the three virtues – Justice, Strength and Temperance – though these changes have little influence on the allegory. The one card that is constantly in the same position in all the known orders is Death, which is number 13. Because Death is clearly near the middle of the deck and not at the end where we might assume it would be, this indicates that the story in the trumps is a mystery of death and rebirth (it also demonstrates that number symbolism is incorporated). Alchemy, as the main channel of the mysteries to have survived, would be the most likely inspiration for this aspect of the cards.

The cards which in English are called the Hierophant and the High Priestess are called the Pope and the Popess (also Papess) in the original decks. This pairing of the Pope with a female partner would be considered heretical, and could not come from an orthodox source. It is more likely to come from alchemy, which strongly strives for a balance of the masculine and feminine (many texts even stipulate that the male alchemist must work with a female partner, called his mystical sister or *soror mystica*). Other examples of this pairing in the Tarot can be seen in the Emperor and Empress, and the inclusion of the Queen in the court cards. The minchiate of Florence (their name for their variation of the Tarot) even replaces the jack with a lady in two suits, and includes in its trumps an additional four cards representing the elements – an unmistakable alchemical addition.

The last two cards, Judgement and the World, sometimes switch places in different orders, but their alchemical significance is not changed. Judgement symbolizes the revival of dead matter, which is the goal of the opus, and the World clearly is the Anima Mundi. The majority of printed World cards from the 1400s show an androgynous angel (spirit) holding or standing on a circle containing a landscape (earth). A variation dating from *circa* 1500, which is now in a collection in Paris, depicts Hermes on top of a circle which has been divided into four compartments, each of which contains a depiction of one of the elements – another unmistakable alchemical design.

The familiar nude centred between symbols of the four evangelists, which were traditionally equated with the four elements, is a symbol of the Anima Mundi as *quinta essentia*. This image seems to have developed in France in the late 1500s, and became the standard design on the Tarot of Marseilles. A single variation from France, dated

Hermes as World,
circa *1500*

Seventeenth and eighteenth century French World cards

circa 1650, portrays Christ in the centre of the symbols of
the evangelists. He is holding a sceptre and wearing a cape,
but otherwise he is nude (symbolizing the naked truth).
There are several other world cards from this time with the
same image, except that the nude with the sceptre and cape
is female. This female Christ seems to represent the Gnostic
Sophia, the male Christ's feminine counterpart, and another symbol of the Anima Mundi.

The best evidence for the alchemical connection, however, is the *Alchemical Tarot* deck itself, which combines alchemical and Tarot symbols on each card.

By the late eighteenth century Tarot cards were still used primarily for games. At about this time these curious-looking cards caught the attention of occultists, who immediately seized upon them as books of secret learning. Most of the theories were more fanciful than factual. Ironically, one of the most popular theories held that the cards were esoteric Egyptian wisdom, which came remarkably close to the truth, considering the Egyptian origins of Western alchemy.

The Egyptian connection was conceived by Antoine Court de Gebelin (1725–84), a French archaeologist, Egyptologist and high-ranking Freemason. Gebelin said the Tarot symbols were fragments of an ancient Egyptian book, the *Book of Thoth*. Thoth – portrayed as having either the head of an ibis or a baboon – was the god of magic, writing, healing, arithmetic, astrology and alchemy, who created the universe and transmitted his wisdom to mankind. As already mentioned, the Greeks equated Thoth with Hermes, the god of alchemy.

Gebelin said he stumbled upon the Tarot and uncovered its Egyptian origins by accident while calling upon an unnamed countess. He visited her at her home, and found her playing a game with Tarot cards. When she laid out the World card, Gebelin said, he immediately recognized it as an Egyptian allegory that had survived the ravages of time in this humble form.

Gebelin said that the word 'tarot' was derived from two Egyptian words, *tar*, meaning 'road', and *ro*, meaning 'royal' (his 'translation' of two alleged Egyptian words preceded the discovery of the Rosetta Stone, which would prove his assertion false). The Tarot, he said, represented the 'royal road' to wisdom. Furthermore, the 22 trumps were representations of 22 stone tablets hidden in a temple that at one time had sat between the paws of the Great Sphinx, but had long ago disappeared into the sands. The cards were either allegories of Egyptian philosophy and religion expressed in hieroglyphics or told the history of the world, beginning with Mercury (Hermes or Thoth).

According to Gebelin, the Egyptians devised a card game with the Tarot, which they passed on to the Romans during the early Christian centuries. The game remained within Italy until the end of the Holy Roman Empire. The cards were dispersed throughout Europe by the Gypsies, who had saved all that was left of the Ancient Egyptian writings, and used the cards for fortune telling. Historians now know that the Gypsies originated in India and not in Egypt, and that their arrival in the West was too late to spread the cards.

Gebelin's theory, published as part of his nine-volume book, *Le Monde Primitif* (1773–84), had an enormous romantic appeal and became quite popular, despite the fact that it was never substantiated. Nonetheless, fortune-tellers and occultists reiterated the story, even long after the Rosetta Stone was found (in 1799) and deciphered (in 1821). Inspired by Gebelin, the Parisian occultist Etteilla created his own Tarot, designed solely for divination. Although he is considered an opportunist, Etteilla did much to popularize this use of the Tarot.

In the nineteenth century occultists looked for other connections to the Tarot, such as the Kabbala. One of the chief proponents of this approach was Eliphas Levi (1810–75), the pseudonym of Alphonse Louis Constant, a French philosopher, occultist and an Abbé of the Roman Catholic Church, who helped revive interest in ritual magic.

Eliphas Levi (a shortened version of Constant's name in Hebrew, which he adopted for occult purposes) equated the 22 trumps (which he called 'keys') to the 22 letters in the

Hebrew alphabet in order to 'prove' that it was the perfect tool for divination. This correlation of symbols works at times, but mostly it is forced and unconvincing. The link between the Kabbala and the Tarot is not direct, as Levi argued. Instead, it comes through the Renaissance revival of Neoplatonic syncretism, which included both the Kabbala and alchemy.

Perhaps the greatest modern figure to interpret the Tarot was Arthur Edward Waite, a Freemason and a member of the Hermetic Order of the Golden Dawn, which was probably the most well-known magical order of modern times. The Golden Dawn flourished briefly in the late nineteenth and early twentieth centuries, and included as members some of the most prominent occult and literary figures of the day, such as Aleister Crowley, William Butler Yeats, Samuel Liddell Macgregor Mathers, Dion Fortune and others. The Golden Dawn followed in Giordano Bruno's footsteps by using Tarot images in magical meditations and contemplations as gateways and guides to various levels in astral projection. Use of the images helped the astral traveller to avoid wandering along the astral byways, and kept the initiate on track.

Waite reinterpreted the Tarot cards according to what he believed were their original mystical meanings. Tarot cards themselves did not predate the fourteenth century, he said, but they employed much older symbols. In designing his own Tarot deck, Waite drew upon his knowledge of the Hermetic Kabbala and alchemy. The cards were drawn by a fellow member of the Golden Dawn, Pamela Colman Smith, an artist with psychic abilities, and the deck was published in 1910. According to Waite the card symbols were 'gates which opened on realms of vision beyond occult dreams'. The trumps were named the Major Arcana (major secrets), the four suits with pip and court cards were named the Minor Arcana, and – for the first time – each card in the

Minor Arcana had its own pictorial image and not just suit symbols, which made them much more useful in meditation and divination.

Recently the Tarot field has seen an explosion of variations of deck themes and executions. Regardless of imagery, the alchemical content of the Tarot remains: the cards serve as gateways to higher planes, and they light a spiritual path to cosmic consciousness.

2
BASIC CONCEPTS
OF ALCHEMY

As we noted in the previous chapter, descriptions of the alchemical process vary considerably from alchemist to alchemist, due to the highly personal nature of their respective visions. However, most alchemists agree on several basic concepts and principal stages of the opus, which are framed by a mystical, mathematical system of number symbols derived from Pythagoras. The numbers 1, 2, 3 and 4 are particularly significant, as can be seen in the following quotation from a sixteenth-century alchemical text, the *Rosarium Philosophorum* (p. 42):

> Make a round circle out of the man and woman, and draw out of it a quadrangle, and out of the quadrangle a triangle, make a round circle, and thou shalt have the Stone of the Philosophers.

These basic concepts are expressed throughout the Alchemical Tarot, so it is important to understand them. Let us take a look at them.

One: Primal Unity

The number one in alchemy is represented by the *prima materia*, the single, invisible, indestructible substance that Aristotle said was the alpha and omega of all matter; everything originates from the *prima materia*, and everything eventually returns to it. This is symbolized in alchemy by the *ouroboros*, a serpent that forms a circle by bringing its tail to its mouth.

The alchemists believed *prima materia* to be a living soul. As mentioned in Chapter 1, this substance was known by various names, including the Anima Mundi, the *quinta essentia* and the Unus Mundus. Ruland's *Lexicon of Alchemy* lists 134 different definitions for the *prima materia*, many of which contradict each other. For example, it is called a medicine, meaning a panacea, and yet it states that 'there is no stronger poison in the world'. Alchemists also called the initial substance that would become the subject of the opus the *prima materia*. Although in this raw state, the Anima Mundi was not yet released.

In the Alchemical Tarot we find the *prima materia* expressed in the Magician and the World cards. The Magician is the *prima materia* in the beginning of the opus; the World is the *prima materia* at the culmination of the opus.

In the World card the *prima materia* has several expressions. It is the Anima Mundi, or world soul, depicted as a woman with a numinous glow, whose nudity symbolizes that she is the uncovered truth. It is the *quinta essentia*, depicted in the quincunx, an arrangement of five objects in a square with one object at each corner and the unifying element in the middle (like the number five on a die). It is the Unus Mundus, or the world of the one, symbolized by the design that unifies many images into one circular diagram (in fact, the circle alone may be used as a symbol of the Unus Mundus).

In Jungian terms the initial *prima materia* refers to the unconscious. In its primal state before creation the *prima materia* is called the *massa confusa*, or the chaos on which the world of form was imposed (the *massa confusa* relates to the Fool card and the Magician is the world of form).

Likewise, the unconscious, when first encountered, seems confusing and illogical until the order of consciousness is imposed on it. The philosopher's stone has the power to bring whatever it is combined with back into a preformed state, so that its form may change or transform. This is also the goal of the psyche itself, which seeks to dissolve fixed aspects of the personality back into their undifferentiated state, so that they can transform into the higher state Jung called individuation. Individuation corresponds to the *prima materia* as Anima Mundi.

Two: Duality

A fundamental duality of masculine and feminine forces permeates all alchemical material. This duality can be seen in various pairs of symbols: mercury and sulphur, white and red, volatile and fixed, moon and sun, king and queen. These symbols of duality appear throughout the Alchemical Tarot.

The *ouroboros* has been mentioned as a symbol of unity, but alchemists realized that duality emerges out of unity, and the *ouroboros* symbolizes this aspect as well. One of the oldest renditions of the *ouroboros* in alchemy can be found in a third-century Coptic manuscript. This same distinctively shaded *ouroboros* was included in the eleventh-century *Codex Marcianus*. To express the emerging duality the upper half of this *ouroboros* is black and the lower half is white. If we think of the head as eating the tail, then the

Codex Marcianus ouroboros

upper half is life and the bottom death, but death continually leads to rebirth as it sustains the head. If the white tail is thought of as a phallus entering the feminine black upper half, then its life-renewing power stems from the sexual generation of its two parts.

A tenth-century Arab text, *De Chemia*, by Mohammed ibn Umail, describes a statue of Hermes Trismegistus presenting in his hands an engraved tablet revealing the secrets of alchemy. On the tablet are various symbols of duality, including several variations of the sun and moon, and the two birds described in the following quotation from that text:

> Looked at schematically, the birds would be lying one over the other, each with its head to the tail of the other bird, one being winged and the other wingless. It was as though they wanted to fly together, or as though the wingless one was keeping the other back, that is the upper bird wanted to carry away the lower, but the lower bird held it back and prevented it from flying away. The two birds were bound together, were homogeneous and of the same substance and they were painted in one sphere as though the image of two things in one. (*Alchemy*, p. 109)

In this image of a winged and a wingless bird swallowing each other's tails, we can see another form of the *ouroboros*. The two halves have become separate beings which devour each other. In later alchemical texts they take the form of two serpents or dragons, representing the volatile (winged) and the fixed (wingless). These dragons can be seen on the Wheel of Fortune card in the Alchemical Tarot.

The alchemical opus demands that the *prima materia* (the *ouroboros*) be cooked so that the fixed and volatile separate. They are then transformed into one another, in cycle after cycle, until they are purified.

> That which is volatile may be fixed of them by the means of policies but from hence that which is fixed may be made volatile, and again volatile fixed, and in this order the most precious secret is accomplished.
>
> (*Rosarium Philosophorum*, p. 90)

The tenth-century Arabic alchemist Senior says that this wingless, fixed bird is red sulphur (masculine) and that the winged, volatile bird is the soul (feminine). We may consider the fixed as the liquid, which is being cooked, and the volatile as the vapour rising from the boiling substance. The vapour must be captured and condensed so that it can be revaporized in a continuous process called distillation. Alchemists would patiently distil a substance numerous times before it was purified enough for further operations.

Jung describes sulphur as an active, corrosive, evil-smelling substance; in folklore it is equated with the devil, who is described as leaving a sulphurous smell. However, in alchemy, sulphur is the lover of the bride, and is equated with the sun. These conflicting qualities successfully depict the driving, emotional, psychic life force called the libido.

Depression, as viewed by Jung, is a natural process of the psyche. He described it as an introverted psychic state in which the imagination churns to bring out hidden fears and fantasies. If allowed its full course, it leads to an integration of this material, and to calmness and understanding.

This is the natural process that psychoanalysis duplicates, and it is analogous to the alchemical cooking of the sulphur (producing the libido) to extract the vapour (fantasies). The process must be performed numerous times to approach a state of psychic wholeness, and find the true creative purpose behind the libido's seemingly demonic demands.

In later alchemical literature the masculine and feminine become personified as a king and a queen, who are brother and sister, as well as lovers. The sixteenth-century *Rosarium*

Philosophorum contains a series of 20 illustrations, which at the start depict the king standing on the sun and the queen on the moon. In subsequent pictures the couple disrobe, enter a bath together and engage in sexual intercourse. This prolonged intercourse leads to a merging of their two bodies, until they leave the bath as a winged hermaphrodite, standing on the moon. The process is repeated, and once again they emerge as a winged herm-aphrodite, this time surmounting a three-headed serpent.

The king and queen correspond to Jung's animus and anima, archetypes of masculine and feminine psychic forces in the unconscious. As mentioned in Chapter 1, the animus represents the male element in the psyche of a woman, and the female figure would represent her ego. In a man the female would represent the anima and the male figure his ego. Both are sources of inner convictions and fantasies that can be unreasonable or destructive (sometimes the anima is referred to as a *femme fatale* and the animus as a Bluebeard). They can also be benevolent inner guides or beacons, leading one into the unconscious and to the Higher Self. They often appear in dreams as lovers or beckoning guides.

In the Alchemical Tarot we see the union of the king and queen in the Lovers card, and a resulting hermaphrodite in the Devil card, but the second and greater union is repre-sented by the Sun card.

Three: Triplicity

The integration of the ego with the unconscious can be sym-bolized as a marriage or union with the animus or the anima, which can lead to the hermaphrodite, an image of the Higher Self. With the introduction of the Higher Self, the alchemical couple now develop a third force, which completes the triangle mentioned earlier in the quotation from the *Rosarium*. The theme is further expanded in the following quotation from the *Rosarium* (*Alchemy: an Introduction to the Symbolism and the Psychology*, pp. 126–8):

> Philosophy hath three parts: Sol, Luna, and Mercury.

Gnostics claimed there were three parts to an individual: body, spirit (mind), and soul. In Jabir's eighth-century symbolism, sulphur is masculine (spirit) and mercury is feminine (soul); European alchemists later added salt (the body) to Jabir's pair. By comparing the above quotation, however, we can see that the gender of the chemical symbols can differ greatly from one text to another – particularly that of mercury. Here mercury is clearly the hermaphrodite or the Higher Self which is both masculine and feminine.

In mythology Mercury (Hermes in Greek), as messenger of the divine world, was able to take on any form; therefore, he was able to change his sex, making him a manifestation of the anima, animus, or both. Priests of Hermes in Cyprus wore artificial breasts and women's clothing, similar to the practice of Siberian and Eskimo shamans. This may be interpreted as the priests' attempt to identify with their anima, and thereby make contact with the unconscious, or as their identification with the hermaphroditic god. The word 'hermaphrodite' itself is a combination of the name of Hermes with his sometime lover, Aphrodite, suggesting a sexual connection similar to the images in the *Rosarium*.

Mercury, as a symbol, is as quick and elusive as the god himself. In another quote from the *Rosarium*, we can see that even in the same text his meaning changes from one statement to another:

> The Body is Venus and the Woman; The Spirit is Mercury and the Man; the Soul is Sol and Luna. The Body must melt into first matter which is mercury.
>
> (*Rosarium Philosophorum*, p. 26)

Here the body refers to the physical, which is seen as feminine. Mercury, the spirit – which in the sixteenth century referred to what we would call the mind – is masculine. The soul (self), being hermaphroditic, is seen to have a masculine and a feminine part symbolized by the two luminous bodies. By differentiating them we see that four parts can be drawn out of the three.

Four: The Quadrangle

Aristotle's theory postulates that all matter is composed of four elements extracted from the *prima materia*: earth, air, fire and water. These four elements are ubiquitous in the ancient world, being almost identical in Europe, Asia, Africa, and even the Americas (in China there were five: water, fire, wood, metal and earth). The number four in general is associated with the world and physical reality, which has four directions, four dimensions and four seasons.

Aristotle carried the concept a step further, by introducing the four qualities: dry, moist, hot and cold. Each element possesses two qualities: earth is dry and cold, water cold and wet, air wet and hot, and fire hot and dry. As can be seen, one quality is shared by any two successive elements; therefore, each element can be transformed into another element that shares the same quality by manipulating the unshared quality. It was thought that in this way a substance could be changed from one element to another in a continuous circle. Aristotle's theory was the basis for the alchemical belief in the possibility of the transformation of one material into another.

Now, returning to Jabir's theory, we can see that his two components comprising metals are actually a variation of the four elements. Earthy smoke is earth becoming fire, as its dryness becomes hot, and watery vapour is water becoming air, as its wetness becomes hot. When these two substances were imprisoned in the earth they became the symbolic components, sulphur and mercury, which combined in differing proportions with varying amounts of impurities to make all metals. Only if they were pure and in correct balance would they make gold. Therefore, the alchemists thought they could make gold by removing the impurities from other metals.

Alchemical Stages

In alchemy there is a quadruple set of colour symbols: these four stages can be traced to the oldest-known alchemist, Zosimos. This set of symbols outlines the process of the opus (also called a year because it had four stages or seasons), depicting each stage as a colour. The stages and colours are sometimes paired with the four elements. The stages are, in order, the nigredo (the blackening), the albedo (the whitening), the citrinitas (the yellowing) and the rubedo (the reddening).

In the first stage, the nigredo, the initial substance which is placed in the alchemist's oven (*athanor*), is separated into its elements by dissolution (*solutio*), division (*divisio*), or separation (*separatio*). The male and female parts are then reunited in the sealed retort or vessel (the *coniunctio*, *matrimonium*, or *coitus*). Then the product of the union is reduced to ash (the *calcinatio*), killed (the *mortificatio*), and blackened (the *putrefactio*). In the *putrefactio* a substance is created that is 'blacker than black', and the nigredo is complete. This completion is represented by the Devil card in the Alchemical Tarot.

The albedo is a process of whitening the black substance by washing (the *baptisma*, or *ablutio*). When the albedo is complete, the alchemist often starts all over again, reblackening the matter and again washing it white. After many cycles the matter is gradually purified, until the soul (Anima

Mundi) is released from the death of the nigredo and is reunited with the body. This produces a temporary display of many colours (*omnes colores* or *cauda pavonis*) called the 'peacock's tail'. When the matter returns to white the albedo is complete and 'the white that contains all colours' is formed. This is the *lapis albus* or *tinctura alba*, which can transform base metal into silver, the white feminine metal. The *lapis albus* is represented by the Moon card.

The albedo is called the moon; it is also the dawn before the sunrise of the citrinitas, the yellow stage which relates to the Sun card. The citrinitas is a result of raising the heat in the oven, and is a transitional stage leading to the rubedo. By the sixteenth century most texts omitted the citrinitas, or considered it part of the rubedo, reducing the stages from four to three.

In the final red stage the rubedo, the sun of the citrinitas, who is also called the red king (red is the masculine colour), is married to the white lunar queen of the albedo, in a final 'great coniunctio', or 'chemical wedding'. In this way the hermaphroditic philosopher's stone, which has the highest power of transformation, is formed. The World card in our deck represents this final culmination.

Jung felt that the colour stages accurately outlined the process of individuation. The nigredo represents the initial immersion in the unconscious, a process of self-reflection that happens naturally in depression, which is often described as a black mood. When we first encounter the unconscious we are confronted with the aspect that Jung calls the 'shadow', which is that part of our psychic energy that is repressed or neglected. Even beneficial forces, when repressed, become part of the shadow, and at first can appear as demons (the Devil). As we observe and analyse these demons, or use active imagination to transform them, we are purified of their projections, entering a lighter (albedo) state of quiet and peace (the Star). Then we go back to the nigredo and start again. This calmness can be found over and over again, and eventually we learn to keep it.

The albedo's peace, however, is not individuation; there is a danger in the albedo stage of becoming overly analytical and losing spontaneity and drive. As Jung says, we are in need of the red, life-giving blood of the rubedo. The red sulphur demon from the nigredo, which is only a mask over our creative drive and joy of life, must be married with the white peaceful woman of the albedo to achieve the wholeness of individuation.

> Great miracles appear in the hour of conjunction.
> (*Rosarium Philosophorum*, p. 35)

The colours also reflect the three stages of the mystical journey. Black represents the stage of purgation, in which the materialistic ego is broken down. White represents illumination, a cleansing process in which the soul literally 'sees the light'. Red represents union, in which the soul becomes one with the Anima Mundi.

The Major Arcana of the Alchemical Tarot takes us through the alchemical stages, which may be read as the journey to psychic wholeness, or the mystical journey of spiritual illumination.

Seven Metals, Seven Operations

The Ancients recognized seven planets and equated each to one of the seven days of the week. The word 'planet' is derived from the Greek *planētai* (wanderers). The planets were called wanderers because, when viewed with the naked eye, they were the only luminous bodies in the night sky that appeared to move independently from the constellations. They included the sun and moon as well as the presently designated planets of Mercury, Venus, Mars, Jupiter and Saturn.

Aristotle developed a model of the universe with the earth in the centre and each planet on its own crystal sphere ascending away from the earth like layers of an onion. On the eighth sphere were the fixed stars. Aristotle's model was refined by Ptolemy, and became the accepted scientific model for centuries. Copernicus challenged it in 1473 and put the sun in the centre, but his model was no more accurate at predicting the movements of the planets until Kepler refined it in the sixteenth century by adding elliptical orbits.

The earth-centred model of the universe was used by mystics. The ancient mystery religions viewed the planets as a ladder or stairway to heaven, which was thought to be beyond the sphere of the stars. This stair was how the soul ascended after death. The ruling god, or later the archangel or archon, of each planet corresponded to an aspect of the personality; for instance, love, power, anger (this is the origin of the Seven Deadly Sins and the Seven Virtues.) The aspect had to be reconciled when the soul reached that planet in order not to impede its progress to the next level. The purer the soul, the greater its gnosis or its magic ability, and the closer it progressed to heaven. Initiation rites in the mysteries often included an ascent of the ladder of the planets accomplished while in a trance. This mystic ladder was incorporated into the Neoplatonic list of emanations. It often appears in dreams, and in alchemical texts, such as the *Mutus Liber*.

Alchemists in a series of correspondences equated each of the seven known metals to one of the planets and viewed them as a ladder of perfection from lead to gold (the order of the five in between differs from one author to another). This was not just a poetic metaphor; the alchemists felt that each metal was the living essence of that planet on earth. Just as plants and animals are alive, they believed that minerals are alive and reproduced in the earth through a type of sexual interaction. Each living metal, as it is purified in nature, progresses to a higher state until it becomes gold. The alchemists endeavoured to copy and speed up this natural process in their laboratories, and simultaneously purify and refine their souls.

The correlation between the seven planets and the seven metals is shown in the following chart. Their correlation and order of ascent, from the bottom up, is based on Martin Ruland's seventeenth-century *Lexicon of Alchemy*.

Metal	Planet
Gold	Sun
Silver	Moon
Quicksilver	Mercury
Copper	Venus
Iron	Mars
Tin	Jupiter
Lead	Saturn

The Star card in the Alchemical Tarot depicts the mystical ladder of the planets.

In their work alchemists developed numerous chemical operations, many of which had more than one name. These were also seen as a ladder of ascent because of their order in the process of purifying the subject of the opus. Therefore, the principal ones were often placed in ascending lists of seven or 12 (12 is another number of completion, related to the 12 signs of the zodiac, or the 12 months of the year).

The names, order and importance of the operations changed from one alchemist to another. In fact, no two descriptions agree completely. Again, this is primarily due to the alchemists' reliance upon personal and direct revelation. Generally, however, the number of stages is given at between seven and 12, although some names actually refer to a combination of operations and therefore the list can be expanded. The alchemist George Ripley called the stages the Twelve Gates, and likened them to entrances to a circular castle.

For our purposes with the Alchemical Tarot we will use the seven primary operations, given here in a progressive list:

Solutio	Moritificatio
Separatio	Baptisma
Coniunctio	Multiplicatio
Calcinatio	

Here are descriptions of the operations:

Solutio, or solution, literally means to turn a solid into a liquid. In the initial stage the matter of the work is often liquified for further operations. This is accomplished by the coagulated (solid) substance being swallowed by a liquid solvent. For example, gold or silver can be dissolved into mercury to form an amalgamate (this is the basis of the ancient method for extracting gold from ore). Psychologically, the solid can be thought of as the ego consciousness, consisting of fixed ideas, which at this stage is dissolved into the mercury of the unconscious.

Separatio, or separation, is the breaking down of the subject into its elements.

> Reduce your stone to the four elements, unite them into one and you will have the whole magistery.
> (*Tractus Aurens*, in *Psychology and Alchemy*, p. 128)

This is accomplished by various other operations: heating, evaporation, filtration, abstraction, depletion, dilation or removal. The separation into elements is not meant to be literal; it is only a separation of impurities from the subject. Psychologically, it can be described as the analysis and classification of unconscious material.

Coniunctio, or conjunction, is the joining of two substances to make a third. To the alchemist it was a sexual union between the male and female elements of the subjects; it was necessary that they be 'married alive' so that the union would be fruitful. The product could be described as the hermaphrodite or as a child. There are two *coniunctios* in the opus. In the early stages the male and female were not yet purified, so it was necessary for their product of the first *coniunctio* to be put through further operations. The great *coniunctio*, at the end of the work after purification, produced the *lapis* as its product. Psychologically it can be described as a marriage of the ego with the anima or animus, which must happen after the purification of the albedo before it can lead to individuation.

Calcinatio, or calcination, is the chemically executed corrosion or intense heating of the matter, to drive off water, or other volatile constituents, and reduce it to a white ash (*calx*, or chalky dust). The fire or corrosive agent is called 'the dragon who drinks the water'. The word 'calx' means lime, and the process probably stems from the production of quicklime by heating limestone. The *Rosarium* (p. 70) instructs, 'Sow your gold into white foliated earth, which by calcination is made fiery, subtle and airy.' The king (ego) who is killed in the next operation must be buried in this white ground (created by the emotions of the libido intensifying and burning themselves out). In this way the king, as in the sacrifice of a fertility ritual, will multiply like grain as he is reborn.

Mortificatio is the killing of the product of the initial union; this could be the king mentioned above, or it could be the hermaphrodite. It has no modern chemical equivalent, because chemists no longer believe that minerals are alive. This murder is performed so that the matter can be resurrected in a new and exalted form. To be complete, the body must decompose or rot – to become a black substance –

in the second part of the operation called *putrefactio*.

The king can be equated to the ego, who must die so that the emerging self will not be blocked, and so that he will be able to be reborn with this new psychic centre.

> I never saw anything that had life to grow and increase without putrefaction, and vain would the work of alchemy be, unless it were putrefied.
> (*Rosarium Philosophorum*, p. 40)

The *baptisma*, or purification, is a washing or distillation of the black putrefied body so that it is purified and made white (the albedo stage). Like the religious ritual of baptism, it is meant to be a rejuvenating immersion in the womb of primal energies – internally, a death of the old ego and the rebirth of the new self. This process must be repeated until its peace and wellbeing bond to the personality. This operation creates a new substance called mercurial water, or the 'mother of the stone'.

Multiplicatio is an operation that is performed by the philosopher's stone itself once it has been created by the final *coniunctio* of the resurrected king and queen (in the rubedo stage). Now, like a seed that can produce more seeds, after it has sprouted from the earth and matured, the stone purifies whatever it touches and thereby multiplies its perfection. It can transform base metal into gold, and it is the elixir of life. Similarly, when individuation is achieved, this consciousness of the self is contagious, and the individuated person has a transformative, healing influence on others.

> In making known to you all that I have seen and experienced, I am only following the maxim of Seneca, who said that he desired knowledge chiefly that he might impart it to others.
> (*The Hermetic Museum: Restored and Enlarged*, p. 300)

3
THE MAJOR ARCANA

THE Alchemical Tarot is one of the most powerful Tarots you will ever work with. Its Major Arcana is a textbook for the Great Work and each card is a step in the process. The alchemist, represented by the Fool, begins with the *prima materia*, represented by the Magician, and culminates in merging with the Anima Mundi or God consciousness, represented by the World.

To fully understand and appreciate the profound meanings contained in each of these cards, we recommend studying them one by one from start to finish. Alchemical symbols have been joined with Neoplatonic and Tarot symbols. The deck is permeated with nuances and subtleties. Once you grasp how the cards play out the opus or the Great Work, and know where each card is in the process of the Work, then you will be able to master the deck's wisdom in both meditations and readings.

0 THE FOOL

Fools understanding the sayings of the Philosophers according to the letter do find out no truth.

(Rosarium Philosophorum, p. 11)

The Fool represents the neophyte alchemist, who is the beginning of the Work, and ultimately becomes the end of it as well. To obtain the philosopher's stone the alchemist must learn to maintain and balance the adventure, honesty and sincerity possessed by the novice with the wisdom acquired by the adept. In Zen this is called 'beginner's mind'. We must never lose our sense of wonder in the pursuit of truth.

The Fool is blindfolded to signify his ignorance of the basic principles of alchemy. He does not yet comprehend the *prima materia*, the first substance needed for the Work. It exists everywhere, but the Fool does not recognize it or realize its value and, as a result, he risks stumbling about in darkness. The word 'blind' derives from the Indo-European term *bhlendhow*, which means confusion and not knowing where to go. It is related to the word 'blunder', which comes from the Old Norse term *blunda*, meaning to shut one's eyes.

If the Fool could see, he would find the *prima materia* all around him. Since he cannot, it manifests in the form of a hare, a symbol that has profound alchemical, archetypal and shamanistic meanings. In alchemy the hare teaches the axiom, 'visit the interior of the earth and by rectifying thou shalt find the hidden medicinal stone' (from *Musaeum Hermeticum*, translated by A.E. Waite, p. 259). The hare lives in the earth, and is an archetypal guide to the under-world of the unconscious. The animal appears here to guide the Fool down into those depths, into the darkness that must be charted for the Fool to lose his ignorance and re-emerge into the light. It is a shamanistic journey, for the shaman is led by a spirit guide down through a hole in the earth to enter other realms.

In addition to not seeing the hare, the Fool is unaware that he is under divine guidance. The star over his head is the Platonic star that guides every person through life. It is, in Jungian terms, the self. The feathers in the Fool's cap, in the alchemical colours of opposites, function like antennae or sensors for the higher self, dividing the energy into mas-culine and feminine aspects. This guidance functions in spite of the Fool's foolishness, and when he drops his blind-fold he will be able to utilize this guidance much more astutely.

Psychologically, the Fool represents the natural mind. He seeks to find harmony in the universe. He is the beginning and the end, the place where the head of the *ouroboros* bites its own tail, forming the unbroken circle of the cosmos – the cosmic egg. The Fool is the newborn. Thus, the number of his card is zero, which can also be depicted as a circle.

The drawing of the card is based on Steffan Michelspacher's *Cabala* (1616).

Tarot wisdom: The Fool represents ignorance or naiveté but shows us that everything we need to begin our spiritual journey and to initiate change is within our grasp. We begin with the raw material of transmutation ready before us. If we place our trust in a higher order we will be guided through the dangers and darkness and into the light. We need only open our eyes and go forward with both awe and courage. As we gain knowledge we will be transformed.

I

I THE MAGICIAN

Mercury is mentioned everywhere, in every alchemical work, and is supposed to perform everything – Mercury is the subject and matter of the stone.

(*A Lexicon of Alchemy*, p. 229)

The Magician represents no alchemical process because he is the matter of the Great Work itself. He is the Anima Mundi, as is the end result, seen in the World card. He is the tail swallowed by the *ouroboros*. He is *argent vive*, living silver, the basis of all metals. He is the *prima materia*, the subject and first matter of the philosopher's stone, the seminal ingredient in all things. With the *prima materia* we begin our alchemical transmutation.

The Magician is a cosmic principle personified by the god

Hermes (Mercury), whose mysteries of Hermes are complex and deep.

Hermes is the classical god of universal wisdom, magic and skill, especially skill with words. He is the initiator, the god of beginnings, travel, commerce and sales. He is messenger to the gods in heaven and psychopomp, or guide, of the souls of the dead to the underworld. His swift-footedness makes him the god of speed and running, and of athletics. He carries a magical wand, the caduceus entwined by two snakes, which symbolizes the reconciliation of opposites. He is clever, crafty and sly – the trickster who deceives with eloquent words. He is a consort of Aphrodite, goddess of love, with whom he unites to form the hermaphrodite of alchemy.

Hermes, along with his Egyptian counterpart, Thoth, also forms a composite: the legendary Hermes Trismegistus, reputed to be the author of the Hermetical texts that form the foundation of alchemy and the Western mystical tradition. The Hermetic writings, actually written by a number of anonymous authors, contain the axiom, 'As above, so below', which the Magician embodies.

Hermes, as the Magician, is the interface between heaven and earth. What is above in the heavens he manifests below on earth. Thus, he commands and unifies the four elements, and is the power that unifies opposites. He is: matter and spirit, cold and heat, poison and healing, metal and liquid, and masculine and feminine. His signatory colours are the red and white of alchemy, which represent, respectively, the male and female polarities which must be united in perfect harmony to achieve the Great Work.

The card, inspired by images in the *Mutus Liber*, shows Hermes the Magician as the unifying force in the centre of his universe. He stands on a fertile patch of earth (the body), from which grow red and white flowers. Fire (the energy of the soul) springs from the rocks. Behind him is the cool, healing *aqua* of the sea (water is the unconscious, the substance of the soul). The blue sky (air) represents intellect, or spirit.

The Magician wears his magical helmet, its gold colour and wings symbolizing the ultimate enlightenment of the Great Work. His right hand holds up to the macrocosm his magical staff, the caduceus, which in mythology has the power to cure any illness, and to change what it touches into gold. Because of these powers the alchemists found the caduceus a convenient symbol for the philosopher's stone. In this first card the caduceus is green, the colour of beginnings, and it is entwined by red and white serpents, the masculine/feminine opposites united in the eternal cycle of life, death and rebirth. The Magician's left hand points down to the earth, making him a living conduit for cosmic forces to manifest in the earth.

Tarot wisdom: The Magician is a reminder that whatever we see in the manifest world contains a hidden divine essence; therefore, we are not to be taken in by shallow appearances, but must strive for deeper perception. With the Magician we have advanced from the naiveté of the Fool to the awareness of the initiate.

The Magician also represents skill, both physical and verbal. Physical skill relates to athletic prowess, or trade and craft skills, and the Magician plies these with confidence and ease. Verbal skills are the gifts of eloquence and entertainment; however, these skills are also the dark gifts of the trickster who fools and lies with words. Even the most accurate words lie, in the sense that they only point to reality and are not reality itself. If this card relates to something you have been told by others, beware – do not be taken in by eloquence. Stay grounded. Examine and analyse.

The Magician also points to our inner self. In this context

the positive qualities of self-worth and self-confidence are emphasized. Other people are attracted to the engaging, entertaining Magician within you; they admire your skills.

If there are any negative signs in the reading they may point to a tendency to be too intellectual, and to rely too much on left-brain, rational thought. The Magician ideally is a balance of opposites, with the left brain in harmony with the right, matter in harmony with spirit and the microcosm in harmony with the macrocosm.

The Magician's place in the Major Arcana as number one is the position of beginnings. This parallels mythology, for Hermes is the god of initiation and of beginnings. In a reading these beginnings might be a journey, a new spiritual awareness, a new job or a new skill, a new relationship, or a new phase of life. Hermes takes you to the threshold of change but does not lead you across it. That is the next phase of the journey.

II THE HIGH PRIESTESS

Wheresoever we have spoken plainly, there we have spoken nothing, but where we have used riddles and figures, there we have hidden the truth.

(Rosarium Philosophorum, p. 47)*

The image of the High Priestess is influenced by the soror mystica, mystical sister, portrayed in the Mutus Liber, who holds her hand to her lips in a sign of silence. This gesture has been associated with Hermetic philosophy since antiquity, when the Greeks misinterpreted the Egyptian image of the infant Horus sucking his finger, and transformed him into Harpokrates, the god of silence. This card represents the language of silence, and the presence of mystery. It is the truth behind the trickster's verbal illusions, but a truth that can be penetrated only through perseverance.

The High Priestess represents water, which is an archetypal symbol of the unconscious. Sailing in her moon boat on the sea, she becomes the gateway to the deepest parts of ourselves. She acts as the messenger that surfaces from the unseen depths, bringing our inner wisdom to our conscious awareness.

When we attune to the energies of the High Priestess we come into contact with the Great Goddess, who governs the cycles and rhythms of nature – the very mysteries of life. Her moon, which waxes and wanes – the rhythm of life – symbolizes the highest expression of female spirituality; it is the origin of all mystery traditions. She is luna, the feminine aspect of our hermaphroditic soul.

The High Priestess expresses an esoteric spirituality; this is not found in books but comes from direct experience and initiation into the mysteries. Like the mysteries of life hidden in the womb of the Great Goddess, the wisdom of the High Priestess is hidden. Thus, her book is closed, and she is silent. She beckons to lead us to a gnostic, or personally realized, spirituality, but once we are at her gateway we must discover her secrets ourselves by solving her riddles and deciphering her symbols.

The High Priestess begins the alchemical processes called solution and separation; together they are called dissolution. In this process the *prima materia*, symbolized by the Magician, is dissolved and separated into its four elements: water (the High Priestess, feminine soul), earth (the Empress, body), air (the Emperor, spirit/mind), and fire (the Hierophant, masculine soul).

Tarot wisdom: Two is the number of openings, because two halves create a space between each other, as in the image of a doorway. The High Priestess opens the door for us to probe the mysteries that lie beneath our experiences. She encourages us to look for what is hidden – to read between the lines, to find subtleties and nuances. This is the card of intuition, dreams and esoteric knowledge.

III THE EMPRESS

What nature itself has begun, that is brought to perfection by
Art.   *(Rosarium Philosophorum*, p. 28)*

The Empress brings us into contact with another aspect of
the Great Goddess. She is the Mother Goddess, the Earth
Goddess, the embodiment of fertility. She nurtures three
kingdoms in her womb – animal, vegetable and mineral. In
the image here, the child represents the animal kingdom.
The vegetable and mineral kingdoms are represented by the
vegetation and rocks surrounding the Empress.

Alchemically, the Empress represents the alchemical vessel, which nurtures the creation of the philosopher's stone.
She continues the process of dissolution of the *prima materia*, begun by the High Priestess.

The number of the Empress is three, the first complete number, representing a beginning, a middle and an end. In mythology Mother Goddesses are portrayed as having three aspects: virgin, mother and crone, symbolic of birth, life and death. The Mother Goddess creates life, nurtures it, and destroys it, ensuring the unending cycle of all things. The Greeks considered three to be the mother of geometry, because the first figure, a triangle, is comprised of three sides. Thus, the threefold Mother Goddess is the mother of the physical world.

The drawing of the card is inspired by the female figures in *Anatomia auri*, 1628, by Johann Daniel Mylius.

Tarot wisdom: The Empress signifies the potential to attract great abundance and the bounties of life. She is grounded in the earth, and guided by her heart, which helps us to keep our correct centre as we probe the spiritual planes. However, we cannot take this abundance for granted. The alchemical womb must be watched and tended, lest it abort and we be forced to start anew.

IV THE EMPEROR

Use you toward me such devotion of hearing as I shall bring unto you magistery of doctrine and wisdom, for I show to you a true testimony of those things which I have seen with my own eyes and felt with my hands.

(Rosarium Philosophorum, p. 9)

Whereas the Empress is the expression of feminine energy grounded in the physical, the Emperor is the expression of the masculine physical. In addition, he represents the element of air, which in turn symbolizes intellect. Thus, the Empress is the body and the Emperor is the spirit. The term 'spirit' was used during Renaissance times to mean the mind.

The Emperor also represents the ego. He is related to

Apollo, the light of reason. Here he stands aloft on his rock in his element, air. The eagle, sacred to Zeus/Jupiter, the emperor of gods, is testimony to his regal position, and connects him to the heavens.

In alchemy the eagle represents the volatile, which transforms the fixed; it is the agent that has the power to transform matter into its most refined state. The volatile is none other than Hermes/Mercury – the Magician – who is the living spirit of alchemy. Like the Empress, the Emperor continues the process of dissolution of the *prima materia* initiated by the High Priestess.

The Emperor's number, four, is the number of the physical world; there are four seasons, four geographical directions and four elements (air, earth, water and fire). Four symbolizes completeness, solidity and stability. Four also represents the three dimensions of our physical plane with the addition of the fourth dimension of time, and thus establishes the space-time continuum.

The drawing of this card was inspired by the title page of *Anatomic auri*, 1628, by Johann Daniel Mylius.

Tarot wisdom: The Emperor keeps our feet on the ground and stabilizes us. He establishes his firm domain over the physical realm, ruling with thought and intelligence. Yet he is linked to the otherworldly dimensions that must be traversed not in body but in spirit. He keeps us anchored while we penetrate those uncertain frontiers, giving us a lifeline before we feel ready to let loose our earthly bonds and fly.

V THE HIEROPHANT

I behoveth him who would enter into this art and secret wisdom to repel the vice of arrogancy from him, and to become
virtuous and honest and profound in reason, courteous unto
men, merry and pleasant of countenance, patient and a
concealer of secrets.

(Rosarium Philosophorum, p. 24)

As the Emperor plays counterpoint to the Empress, the
Hierophant plays counterpoint to the High Priestess. Hers
is hidden knowledge; his is open. The Hierophant represents fire, and masculine spirituality – the sol or sun aspect
of the soul. The High Priestess, as you recall, represents the
feminine, luna or moon, aspect of the soul.

In the Marseilles Tarot this card is the Pope. The Pope is
the leader of exoteric religion, which creates order and laws

of morality for the masses. The card was changed to the Hierophant by Arthur Edward Waite for the Rider–Waite deck; its name comes from the Greek term *hierophantes*, which is a priest who conducts initiation into the mysteries. In the Tarot the Hierophant explains the mysteries of the cards. His book is open; the secrets are there to be read by all.

The Hierophant is crowned by a magnificent triple crown, which is often seen in alchemical texts and represents dominion over the three kingdoms – animal, vegetable and mineral – which have been nurtured by the Empress. The triple crown especially applies to Hermes Trismegistus, whose name means 'thrice crowned' or 'thrice great' – literally, 'as great as can be'. The Pope also wears a triple crown which symbolizes the three estates of God, or the Trinity.

The small figures at the sides of the Hierophant represent the Emperor and Empress, who are being joined in sacred marriage. They are the earthly representatives of the celestial masculine and feminine principles, the sun and the moon. Mediating between them and their celestial counterparts are two candles, representing the Hierophant's element, fire.

Fire is reiterated in the throne of the Hierophant which forms an upward pointing triangle, the alchemical symbol for fire, and in The Hierophant's robe which is red. The Hierophant's book shows the fixed and the volatile changing into each other, a motif that we will find repeated in the Wheel of Fortune card, further along in the Work.

The triple aspect of the Hierophant is reinforced by the three moons and three suns shown in the book. The brightest sun is the gold of the Work – the philosopher's stone, the enlightenment.

The Hierophant's number, five, adds the fifth element: the quintessence, or *quinta essentia*, also known as ether. The term comes from the Latin word *quintus*, which means 'the fifth'. Unlike the four elements, which are constantly variable, the *quinta essentia* remains unchanging. It holds the other four elements together, and is the nurturing Anima Mundi. Pythagoras said the fifth element is what the stars are made of. It is a spiritual constant, and adds spiritual quality to the physical world. In magic we find the *quinta essentia* expressed in the motif of the pentagram.

The image on the card is based on the Hermes Trismegistus depicted in *De chemia*, by Senior, in Mangetus, *Bibliotheca chemica curiosa*, 1702.

Tarot wisdom: The Hierophant tells us to let virtue be our guide in our quest of the Work. We are grasping the marriage of the principles of heaven and earth, spirit and matter, masculine and feminine – a union necessary for the synthesis of the philosopher's stone. We are in touch with both those energies, and are capable of keeping them in balance. However, we have much yet to learn, for we are not quite a quarter of the way towards our final goal, the World. The Hierophant's book is open, but it is long and deep. We must integrate the knowledge we have acquired, and continue our quest, for we stand at the threshold of the next major phase of the alchemical process. The Hierophant marks the end of the *solutio*, the dissolution of the *prima materia* into its four elements.

VI THE LOVERS

By themselves they are dissolved and by themselves they are brought together, that they which are two, may be made one body.

(Rosarium Philosophorum, p. 35)

With the Lovers the dissolution of the *prima materia* is complete, and recombination back into unity occurs. Alchemically, the Lovers mark the first or lesser conjunction of the masculine and feminine principles, symbolized by the union of the Emperor and the Empress, with their spiritual essence, Sol and Luna, in the background. This is called the alchemical wedding, and was depicted in the alchemical texts as a wedding ceremony, or more often as a consummation of the marriage.

The scene depicted on early Tarot cards consistently shows lovers, with or without a priest (the figure of the priest on this card in the Marseilles deck is often misinterpreted as another woman), and presided over by Cupid with his bow. This arrangement is directly based on traditional Renaissance betrothal portraits, and clearly represented romantic love, or marriage.

The Lovers' number, six, is sacred to Aphrodite, the goddess of love. The Pythagoreans called six androgynous, because it is both feminine and masculine, and referred to it as the number of marriage. Six is also the first perfect number, because it is the sum of the first three integers. One plus two plus three equals six, and one times two times three equals six. In this way it combines the first odd (masculine), and the first even (feminine) numbers with the primary unity.

Tarot wisdom: The Lovers card signifies joy, the fulfilment of our desires, sensual pleasure, and ideally a balance between the male and female aspects of our personalities. The Lovers are in harmony with each other, and therefore with the entire physical world, but until more depth is gained their harmony can be disrupted by the natural tendencies of desire.

VII THE CHARIOT

When it (the matter of the work) is in the vessel and feels the Sun or the heat incontinently and breathes and evaporates away into the form of most subtle fume, and ascends into the head of the vessel, and this they have called Ascension and Sublimation.

(Rosarium Philosophorum, p. 106)

In the Chariot we find the progeny of the Lovers – their son – who we see setting off on his alchemical journey – a hero's journey. He is brimming with youthful energy and drive, but this energy needs to be focused and directed. The charioteer is likely to go charging off in the wrong direction, or go too fast and burn out his horses. With a vision of his goal before him, he realizes that he must ascend to reach it, but like Phaethon this ascension will lead to an inverted plunge into the underworld.

Phaethon was the son of Helios, the god who drove the sun chariot through the sky. To provide proof of his divine origin, Phaethon convinced his father to let him drive the mighty chariot for a day. Alas, it was a fatal move. He was too immature to handle the immense power of the steeds. Losing control, he veered perilously close to the earth, scorching fields, and drying rivers. To avoid catastrophe, Zeus had to intervene. He struck the rash youth with a thunderbolt, causing him to fall head first into the river Eridanus.

Alchemically, the charioteer has been heated by the energy of the sun, and begins to rise. The vision before him is the solar wheel, or wheel of the year (the opus was often referred to as a year). On the rim of this wheel are images of 19 consecutive sun rises. Nineteen is a number of completion and returns to the one (1+9=10, 1+0=1). Appropriately, 19 is also the number of the Sun card, on which the sun will reappear after Phaethon's descent into the underworld. In the centre of the wheel, suspended by the alchemical trinity of mercury, salt and sulphur, is the spiritual sun. This is not the astronomical sun, but the sun at the centre of our being: the self.

The alchemical process the charioteer represents is sublimation. In sublimation a substance, when heated, goes directly into gaseous state, bypassing liquefaction, and ascends to the top of the alchemical vessel, where it condenses. Sublimation is an improvement in quality – but the alchemist must not be hasty about the process.

The Chariot marks the beginning of the ascension on the Wheel of Fortune. The signature of the chariot is a bold 'I shall reign.'

Seven is the first number of completion. There are seven metals, seven planets, seven days of the week. Hippocrates said our lives have seven seasons divided into seven-year cycles, which are marked by transitions between. In myth, seven is associated with the hero, especially the solar hero (the seventh day is Sunday). Seven is a lucky number, and relates to the hero who is lucky as well as plucky. Plato said the universe is generated out of the triangle and the square, which give the three and the four, the elements of the number seven. One may construct four figures out of the triangle and square: a pyramid (fire), octahedron (air), icosahedron (water) and cube (earth). Seven also is the number of magical and mystical wisdom.

The image on the card here is based on engravings in Johann Daniel Mylius's *Opus Medico-Chymicum* (1618).

Tarot wisdom: The Chariot represents impatience. Alchemical heating is a gradual process – the alchemist should not add too much heat too quickly. As we draw closer to the Stone, we glimpse it, and want to get to it as quickly as possible. It has been hidden from view, and now it is in plain sight. But getting there, to spiritual wholeness, is not a fast process. We must check our impulse to charge off, and proceed more slowly and carefully. We must stay centred.

The Chariot offers us exuberance, energy, ambition, and willingness to take on a challenge. These are good traits that can serve us well, as long as they are properly managed and tempered. The long-distance traveller knows how to pace himself so as not to burn out before reaching his destination.

VIII JUSTICE

Whosoever is ignorant in the weight let him not labor in our books. *(Rosarium Philosophorum, p. 37)*

Prophetically, the first of the three feminine powers encountered by the charioteer is Justice, who is the death aspect of this triple goddess. Justice can be traced back to the Egyptian goddess Maat, who weighs the souls of the dead, and is the embodiment of truth and justice. To the Egyptians Maat was the equivalent of cosmic consciousness or the Tao, the eternal truth from which all things sprang, and to which all things returned. To the Greeks fate was ruled by the three Moirai, but it also had a less familiar dual nature. Tyche ruled over the first part as the goddess of luck and good fortune. Nemesis, the goddess of justice, or divine vengeance, ruled the other half. Nemesis' symbol is the wheel of the year, which shows her connection to the Latin Fortuna. The Romans named this aspect of Fortuna, Libra, and placed her symbol, the balance, at the midpoint of the zodiac, where it marked the autumnal equinox. Our modern image of Justice came into focus in the Renaissance, with her scales of impartial judgement, and her sword which represents the powers of mercy and vengeance.

Alchemically, Justice weighs fire and water; she balances the masculine and feminine principles. Her alchemical process is called disposition, in which the correct proportion of these elements are determined by weight before they are sealed in the retort. The hilt of her sword bears the alchemical symbol for vitriol or 'oil of glass', which is the secret fire.

The image on the card also has a Kabbalistic meaning: it forms the three pillars of the Tree of Life. Justice's impartial scales coincide with the pillar of severity, and her upraised sword with the pillar of mercy. Her body itself forms the central pillar, which connects with the divine presence, rising like smoke beyond our comprehension. The ten eminations, called sephirot, can be appropriately positioned on her body, with Keter on her crown, and Malkut at the base of her torso. (*See the Tree of Life diagram on page 114.*)

Justice's number, eight, is a second or higher order of the number four and represents the balancing of the physical world.

The drawing of this card is based on images from Michael Maier's *Tripus Aureus*, 1618.

Tarot wisdom: Justice reminds us that right action should be based on sound judgement and truth. We must balance objectivity, symbolized by her scale, with subjectivity, symbolized by her sword. This balancing also is demonstrated in the composition of the card. Justice is structured (logic, objectivity), but she stands at the edge of water (intuition, subjectivity). In a higher spiritual sense Justice is the weigher of souls. She assesses our progress along the path of our work, and judges our actions.

The divine fire in her crown, the eye of God, and the rising smoke tell us that in Justice there are subtleties that are beyond our grasp. Sometimes, in the end, we must simply give her our trust.

IX THE HERMIT

By great diligence and labor, and continuance of earnest meditation thou may be raised up into it.

(Rosarium Philosophorum, p. 90)

With the Hermit, the male progeny, now older and wiser, reaches the top of Fortune's wheel, and announces, 'I do reign.' This figure in early Tarot decks was Saturn, the heavy and dour god of time. In Classic myth Saturn devoured his children, as time devours all children, and as his symbol, the *ouroboros*, devours its own tail.

Over time in the Tarot Saturn's hourglass was transformed to a lantern, and the god became a wandering philosopher, the holy hermit. This hermit was likely to have been modelled after the Christian ascetics, who were popular figures during the Middle Ages, and on the story of the Greek philosopher, Diogenes, who, with his lantern in hand, wandered searching for an honest man.

Several alchemical texts depict the early Christian hermit, Morienus (d. 704), who was also an alchemist, and taught this art to the Arabs. The drawing of this card is inspired by these images and by the title page from *The Musaeum Hermeticum* (1625), which depicts a Diogenes-like philosopher following nature's footprints.

In alchemy Saturn represents lead, and rules the nigredo, the dark phase that he journeys through in the trumps. This is signified on this card by his black companion, the raven. His alchemical process is exaltation, in which the *prima materia*, now recombined and balanced, is dissolved into a purer or higher degree of itself. This process is another aspect of the *ouroboros* symbol. It is also an analogy for meditation, the Hermit's practice, which can be described as a turning inwards to raise consciousness.

Nine, the Hermit's number, signifies completion and wisdom. Nine is three cubed, and hence relates to the thrice great, Hermes Trismegistus, founder of Hermetic philosophy. Nine is the end of the natural integers, and thus marks the completion of a cycle.

Tarot wisdom: The search for truth can be a long and solitary journey. When the path is not clear, we may wander a bit, but we have divine light to guide us. We have come a long way on our path, and are at the end of a segment of the journey. Now it is time for solitude, meditation and introspection. We must turn inwards to examine where we have been and gain perspective. We must integrate the wisdom we have acquired during our journey.

X THE WHEEL OF FORTUNE

That which is volatile may be fixed of them by the means of policies, but from hence that which is fixed may be made volatile, and again volatile fixed, and in this order the most precious secret is accomplished which exceeds all secrets of secrets of this world.

(Rosarium Philosophorum, p. 90)

Like many themes in the cards, the medieval image of the Wheel of Fortune predates the Tarot. Because the church favoured its moralistic message, it was a common symbol painted in manuscripts and on church walls. On this card in one of the oldest known Tarot decks, painted by Bonifacto Bembo, *circa* 1450, the winged goddess, Fortuna, can be seen in the centre of her wheel surrounded by four male figures who appear to be rising and falling with the revolutions of the wheel. Each of the men has a scroll emerging from his mouth (or in the case of the man on top, from his orb) which contains his lines in this play. The ascending figure, with ass's ears, declares, 'regnabo' ('I will reign'); the man on top, seated with ass's ears and a mace and orb, states, 'regno' ('I do reign'); descending the wheel head first, a man with an ass's tail bemoans, 'regnavi' ('I have reigned'); and, finally, an old man crawling on the bottom attests, 'sum sine regno' ('I am without reign'). The early printed decks retained these four figures, sometimes transforming them into animals. By the time the Marseilles deck was created these figures had been reduced to three monkeys, still bearing accessories such as ass's ears, and a crown.

This medieval goddess of fortune would be familiar to the ancient Romans, who named her Fortuna, a title that Robert Graves says was derived from the Etruscan goddess Vortumna. Vortumna's name means 'she who turns the wheel of the year'. This reference to the zodiac demonstrates that her wheel is meant to be more than a simple moral warning; it indicates that she is the triple goddess of time and fate, whose cycles of birth, life, death and rebirth were emulated in all ancient mystery traditions.

The Greeks called the three Moirai, or Fates: Clotho, Lachesis and Atropos. Clotho is the goddess of birth, and with her distaff she spins the thread of life. Lachesis is the goddess of chance and luck, who measures the thread. Atropos is the inescapable goddess of destiny, and she cuts the thread. The Romans honoured Fortuna with many names, but three of them – Fortuna Primigenia, Bona Fortuna and Mala Fortuna – seem to relate to these three aspects.

The four male figures on her wheel represent the birth, death and rebirth of the sacred king, a myth that in early times was associated with the waxing and waning of the moon, and later came to describe the adventures of a solar hero.

In the Tarot the cards immediately surrounding the Wheel of Fortune express in detail its theme. The three females, representing three cardinal virtues instead of the more traditional four, can now be seen as the triple goddess of fate. Strength is the young virgin aspect; Temperance, the sustainer of life; and Justice, the goddess of death and rebirth. Likewise the four male characters – the Chariot, the Hermit, the Hanged Man and Death – represent the rise and fall of the sacred king on Fortune's wheel.

The image on this card, inspired by Eleazar's *Uraltes Chrymisches Werk*, 1760, is a detailed representation of the double *ouroboros* seen earlier in the book held by the Hierophant. It represents the fixed (the scaly, masculine serpent on the bottom), and the volatile (the winged and crowned, feminine serpent on top), each transforming into one another as they swallow each other, tail first, in an unending cycle. Many alchemists believed that this process had to be accomplished over and over again, changing the contents of the retort from gas to solid, and back again, as the work gradually spiralled to completion.

The four elements in the corners refer alchemically to the elementary wheel of the sages. Aristotle postulated that all matter comes from four elements that are extracted from the *prima materia*. Each element possesses two of the four elemental qualities: hot, cold, dry and moist. The alchemists could change one element into another by manipulating the qualities shared between two elements; therefore the elements can turn into one another, again symbolized by a wheel.

The number of the Wheel of Fortune, 10, is associated with fate because it contains all whole numbers and therefore all possibilities. Ten also returns to the one, or Monad (one plus zero equals one), and so 10 also represents the universe, the many forming one total unit. Thus, the Wheel of Fortune is no single alchemical process, but an overview of the whole process, placed in the centre of the trumps. Indeed, the numerical, geometric relationships in this card, based on the first four integers, are a suitable pattern for the entire opus.

Tarot wisdom: What goes up must come down. The rise and fall of fate can seem like an unending trap, but as we move to the centre of the wheel, our ups and downs become less extreme, and finally, at the axle, we can reach the stillness at the centre of our being. From this vantage the fluctuations of the fixed and volatile can be seen as the essential rhythm of life. Like its Eastern counterpart, the yin–yang symbol, this image itself can serve as a subject of contemplation to help in attaining a state of calm. Meanwhile, the fact that everything changes often works in our favour, so this can be considered a card of good fortune.

XI STRENGTH

Many people had attempted to conquer the Lion, but few had succeeded.

(The Parabola of Hinricus Madathanus Theosophus, p. 160)

Following Fortuna as the Wheel of Fortune is Strength, who is an aspect of Fortuna. In medieval art Fortuna was depicted as riding in a lion-drawn cart. Here, Strength rides astride a tamed lion. She is white, like fume or smoke.

Strength is also the virgin aspect of the threefold Great Goddess. The virgin is the only one who can tame the unicorn, a creature interchangeable with the lion in alchemy. Here, the lion represents our untamed animal nature, our libido, and the virgin represents our higher self. The higher self tames the lower animal nature through love. Thus,

Strength holds a flaming heart, the symbol of love. The sun and moon are the higher aspects of the Lovers. They pour the masculine and feminine alchemical fluids into a heart-shaped vessel.

The alchemical process represented in this card is fermentation, part of the process of exaltation exemplified by the Hermit. In the exaltation of matter a ferment is incorporated with the matter, entering into it and bringing it to a higher form – this is an analogy for the soul entering the body.

The green lion refers to antimony. The alchemist Valentine noted that antimony has the ability to free gold from impurities, and concluded that it had the innate power to have a similar effect on humankind. Antimony is also the best source of mercury, but it is young and imperfect. Thus, green is the colour of beginnings. He also wrote, in *The Triumphal Chariot of Antimony*, that antimony is poisonous, but can be transmuted into pure medicine.

In numerology the number 11 is considered a master number. One plus one equals two, which is the archetypal feminine principle. Eleven is the Anima Mundi, and in China it is the symbol for the Tao.

The image on this card is based on an illustration in Michael Meier's *Tripus aureus* (1618).

Tarot wisdom: This is a card of inner strength. Our animal nature, our libido, is the source of our strength and vitality, but like the lion it can be dangerous, and demands respect. Like the woman in the illustration, we can tame the lion and make its strength our own; it becomes our mount as we give it direction. But the word 'tame' is misleading, for the woman does not overpower the lion – he has more physical strength than her. Her power, as is ours, is love. She loves the lion, and the lion loves her back; therefore he does her bidding. Power comes when we love our selves, and to love our selves totally we must love our animal selves.

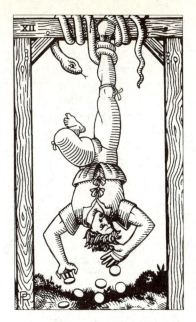

XII THE HANGED MAN

Sow your gold into white foliated earth, which by calcination is made fiery, subtle and airy.

(Rosarium Philosophorum, p. 70)*

The Hanged Man shows the descent on the Wheel of Fortune. He says, 'I did reign.' The fall, however, is not without benefit. The Norse God Odin hung himself upside down on the World Tree, Yggdrasil, in order to obtain wisdom, and Christ hung on the cross – symbolized here by the gallows – to redeem the world. The serpent here is another representation of Christ, according to Gnostic thought.

The alchemical process of the Hanged Man is calcination. In this process matter or a body is suspended over a fire or a corrosive agent to reduce it to white ash. The

Codex Germanicus shows calcination represented by a man hanged from a gallows. The crucified serpent is mercury, which must be sacrificed to complete the Work.

In hanging upside down, the Hanged Man is losing his gold, which represents the loss of worldly possessions, or self-esteem, our sense of our role in the world. In Italy traditionally traitors were hung upside down as a humiliating form of punishment.

The number 12 relates to the months in the solar year, and symbolizes the sacrifice of the solar hero at the year's end.

Tarot wisdom: The Hanged Man represents a fall in terms of our ego or self-image. He may also represent the loss of material belongings. Do not despair, however, for such is necessary in order to transform the lower nature into the higher self. Self-esteem can be repaired, and material objects can be replaced. Perhaps our self-esteem was misdirected; perhaps we did not need so much in the first place. Inevitably, we must go down before we can go up, and while we hang in limbo we can contemplate our errors and determine how to transcend them. The alchemical texts state that the alchemist must sacrifice some gold to make the philosopher's stone.

XIII DEATH

Grind it earnestly until it be possessed with death of the intensity of blackness like dust.

(Rosarium Philosophorum, p. 45)

Death, as a skeleton, stands chained to the alchemical vessel, which has been blackened in the furnace. At the centre is a well-formed nigredo, which is also represented by the raven on Death's shoulder. This is an allusion to Morgana, the Celtic goddess of death, who is accompanied by a raven. The skeleton's arrow is a common attribute of death in medieval pictures. This image is inspired by plate 9 in *Philosophia Reformata*, by Mylius, 1622.

Death is the number 13 in all early Tarots. This is the

number of months in the lunar calendar, and in early myths Death is ruled by the lunar god.

The alchemical processes of Death are mortification and putrefaction, which have no modern chemical counterpart because, unlike the alchemists, scientists no longer believe that chemicals are alive. In putrefaction the composite material is dissolved in heated moisture. One method to accomplish this is to grind up the matter, moisten it and place it in a humid oven. The celestial essence will then separate from its elementary composition. Literally, the matter rots and putrefies.

Tarot wisdom: After we have gone through the fall on the Wheel of Fortune and have finished our suspension as the Hanged Man we are ready for a new beginning. But death is necessary in order to make a fresh start. We must allow the old to pass away so that we can usher in the new. Initiation into the mysteries involves the death of one's old self. We see this necessary death also in the myth of the moon god, who dies every lunar cycle in the new moon and is reborn again. This cycle of death and rebirth is the essential theme of the alchemical process. We go through many deaths in life every time a phase or cycle comes to an end. Jobs, relationships, health, wealth, spiritual growth – all these involve endings and beginnings. The trick of keeping steady on the path is knowing when it is time to let go, and allowing Death to claim what it should. Mourn and give what is passing its due, but do not linger in the grief. Something new is rising on the horizon.

XIV TEMPERANCE

Art imitates nature.
(Rosarium Philosophorum, p. 14)

After Death we enjoy the nurturing of new life, symbolized by Temperance, who is the sustainer of all life. She is the mother aspect of the Great Goddess, who, as one aspect of the Anima Mundi, sustains the world. She is the symbol of time, and her pouring of water from one cup to another represents a clock (before the Renaissance invention of the hourglass the water clock was the most common instrument for measuring time). Temperance has learned to harness the processes and rhythms of nature. Her five-petalled flower is the rose, the symbol of the perfection of the alchemical opus.

The alchemical process of Temperance is distillation. The image on this card is based on Mary the Jewess, the mythical inventor of distillation. She is also known as Bain-Marie, and appears in Michael Meier's *Symbola Aureae mensae* (1617). Distillation is the extraction of material from its solution by forced evaporation. It is the oldest and most fundamental stage of alchemy – the whole process is continual distillation. Hence, Temperance is often called the alchemist.

Duality is expressed in the celestial-terrestrial imagery, in which the water of life flows down from the heavens into her cup, and rises as steam in imitation of the natural process called precipitation. The two streams form an opening shaped like a vagina, which symbolizes the portal of life. Within the opening can be seen the Tree of Life, with five branches each bearing a five-petalled flower. These represent the five senses of humankind, as well as the four elements plus spirit, or the *quinta essentia*.

The number of Temperance is 14, which reduces to five (one plus four equals five), which is the number of perfection on a higher order.

Tarot wisdom: Temperance represents the continual process of life. The key meaning of the card is renewal, a balancing of dual forces, and an achievement of harmony that lies beyond conscious control but simply *is*. Temperance is mistress of nature and its rhythms, and perfection is her goal. She is calm and centred, and maintains her steady rhythm in the face of storms and upheavals. Temperance reminds us that there is a higher order, a higher functioning, to all that happens. We can tune into this higher consciousness by simply concentrating on the present moment, letting go of preconceptions based on the past and not holding expectations for the future.

Temperance is also related to the word 'temper', which means to make strong. Temperance can help our fortitude.

XV THE DEVIL

Instead of a bridal bed and brilliant wedding they were con-
demned to a strong and everlasting prison.

(The Parabola of Hinricus Madathanus Theosophus, p. 164)

The charioteer from the Chariot has now met the Great
Goddess in all three of her aspects – birth, nurturing and
destruction – and dies. He descends to the underworld,
where he is chained to the Devil and transformed into an
image of his parents combined into one being. Similarly,
Hermaphroditus, the son of Hermes and Aphrodite, was
united with the nymph Salmacis to form a dual-sexed being
that was trapped in the Carlan Lake.

The Devil is Hermes/Mercury showing his sinister, ven-
omous side. The Devil is still part of the descent that was

begun with the Wheel of Fortune and which is necessary in order for rebirth to take place on a higher plane.

The Devil here is portrayed by a red dragon on top of the same vessel depicted on the Death card. In the centre of the vessel the substance formed is blacker than black; the goal of the nigredo has been reached.

The dragon is an ancient symbol for the forces of darkness. In the Middle Ages and the Renaissance artists, influenced by biblical descriptions, commonly represented the Christian Devil as a dragon or a serpent. *The Bestiary* from the twelfth century states that, 'The Devil who is the most enormous of all reptiles is like this dragon. He is often borne into the air from his den, and the air around him blazes.' Saturn, the dour and destructive god of time whom we encountered on the Hermit card, is also called a dragon and old serpent, a reference to the *ouroboros* symbol.

The alchemical process of the Devil is coagulation, in which matter is reduced to a solid state in a homogeneous body. That body is comprised of the Lovers, who have united the masculine and feminine principles into the single form of the hermaphrodite. They must now coagulate in darkness while awaiting rebirth. The drawing of the card is influenced by Plate 5 in Mylius Johann Daniel's *Philosophia reformata*.

The number of the Devil is 15, which reduces to six (one plus five equals six), the number of the Lovers.

Tarot wisdom: Gnostic philosophers maintained that matter entrapped spirit, and equated it with evil. The Devil represents this imprisonment – enslavement to our baser instincts and the negative side of our libido, a state that Jung termed the shadow. This can manifest as a state of anger, jealousy, or fear. It can trap us in an addiction. Or, at its worst, it can lead to destruction and violence. However, our libido is also the source of our vitality and strength; it governs our very survival. Our shadow is only that part of ourselves that we have not integrated. It is only evil when it remains unconscious. When we are unaware of this part of ourselves we can project these negative traits against others. Thus, thinking that we are good, and other people evil, we can do our worst. An example of this can be a war, where each side, thinking that goodness and God is with them, unleashes death and destruction on the enemy.

When we make our desires conscious we can choose our behaviour ourselves. We can probe superficial desires, and discover that at the root of desire is the longing for the unity that we call love. When we find this greater source of satisfaction, addictions drop away, as well as the illusion of non-unity.

XVI THE TOWER

When Beast's black hue has vanished in a black smoke, the sages rejoice from the bottom of their hearts.

(The Book of Lambspring, The Hermetic Museum, p. 278)

The Tower represents the oven of alchemy, the athanor, in which the elixir is prepared. Alchemists often referred to their oven as a 'tower', and alchemical art portrayed the oven as a small tower. The images on this card are inspired by the *Philosophia Reformata* (1622) by Mylius Johann Daniel. It shows a triple still, called a *tribikos*, mounted on a small oven. The vessels on top are called alembics, from the Latin name for a stillhead, 'ambix', via the Arabic word 'al-anbiq'.

The alchemical process represented by the Tower is the

second or greater separation, or dissolution. This is a high-er order of the first dissolution, initiated by the High Priestess.

The Tower card represents a breakthrough from the coagulated darkness (nigredo) of the Devil. The darkness is still present in the brooding black of the sky and the grey clouds that ascend from the fire inside the oven. However, the fire has warmed the alchemical solution past the black-ening stage, turning it into a liquified form.

Spiritual illumination in the form of lightning – divine intervention – strikes the oven, cracking it and threatening to destroy it. Simultaneously, the black sky of the nigredo is cut in two by the white light of the second stage, the al-bedo. This is a moment of shattering intensity, at once exhilarating and menacing. If the oven cannot withstand the illumination all may be lost. The power of the strike separates the solution within the tower into the masculine red and the feminine white. The white liquid will form the white stone to make silver; the red liquid will form the red stone to make gold.

For the two figures at the base of the tower the moment is one of enlightenment and exhilaration. The man is the alchemist and the woman the *soror mystica* ('mystic sister'), the female alchemist who is the feminine balance to the masculine polarity that is crucial to the success of alchemy. They are garbed in blue and pale violet, respectively, the colours of the celestial realms. They kneel in positions of exaltation, as though their prayers have been answered by the falling drops. The lightning has opened a gateway to the higher realms, making a ladder of the planets by which souls can ascend to heaven.

The Tower also corresponds to the human body, which, on an esoteric level, is the real alchemical oven. The enlight-enment will be achieved through a sexual-spiritual union.

The number of the Tower, 16, reduces to seven (one plus

six equals seven), which is a magical and mystical number, and is the number of the ladder of the planets which forms the stairway to heaven.

Tarot wisdom: The Tower signifies a breakthrough, a sudden inspiration, a flash of creativity, an opportunity that must be seized. It may also signify an upheaval in life, such as the loss of a job, a change in relationship, or an unexpected move. However, the Tower shows strength; though the athanor is cracked, it does not break. Thus, if the card points to disruption, we can be secure in the knowledge that we have enough security in life and relationships with our immediate family that will enable us to weather the storm successfully.

XVII THE STAR

About the seven stars through whom the divine work is accomplished[:] Senior says in his book in the chapter on the sun and the moon: 'When you have distributed those seven with seven stars and attributed them to the seven stars and then cleansed them nine times til they look like pearls, that is the whitening.'

(Aurora Consurgens, in Alchemy, by Von Franz, p. 220)

The Star is the alchemical process of baptism, the purification in the waters of the unconscious in which the blackness of the Devil is washed away into white.

The baptism is accomplished through Sophia/Aphrodite, also known as Stella Maris, the Star of the Sea, the goddess who like Hermes serves as psychopomp. The inspiration for the illustration on this card comes from alchemical and

Egyptian sources. Basil Valentine's *L'Azoth des Philosophes* features drawings of the 'Siren of the Philosophers' and a ladder of the planets. The Egyptian hieroglyph for star, *sba* or *tua*, which has five starfish-like points, especially denotes the star of dawn or Venus (Aphrodite), and also signifies the hour of morning prayer.

The siren in the Star is Sophia/Aphrodite, who rises as a messenger from the depths of the underworld, or unconscious, represented by the sea. Her tails are spread like a celtic Sheela-na-gig or a Hindu statue of Kali displaying her yoni, representing an open doorway to spiritual transformation through the mysteries of birth, death and rebirth.

Her body is literally the fountain of life. From her breasts pour two streams, one of blood and the other milk; combined with the sea water they form the alchemical trinity of sulphur, mercury and salt. These three liquids are all united in Hermes, who is the water of life, and therefore the fluid which runs through her body.

Above her head is an eight-pointed star encircled by a celestial ladder of seven stars, each on their own sphere. The stars are equated to the planets of ancient astronomy, and are coloured according to their astrologically corresponding gems. This is the same ladder that appears as lightning in the Tower. According to the ancient mystery religions, when the soul dies it ascends through a planetary ladder to heaven. Each planet corresponds to an aspect of the personality, which is reconciled when the soul reaches that particular planet. The further up the soul progresses the more purified it becomes. If the soul is too heavy, or if reconciliation cannot be made at any planet, the soul falls back to earth. The alchemists related each planet to a metal and similarly believed that the metals formed a ladder as each one evolved into its purer essence. Both of these ladders parallel on an internal plane the seven primary chakras of yoga (*see The Alchemical Ladder Spread in Chapter 5*).

Beginning at the top left of the illustration and working anti-clockwise, the planets with their associated gems are:

Mercury	Amethyst
Sol	Topaz
Mars	Ruby
Venus	Emerald
Saturn	Turquoise
Luna	Opal
Jupiter	Carnelian

As in alchemical texts, the order of ascent zig-zags across the picture. The order of the planets with their corresponding evolved metals is shown below, along with the corresponding Tarot cards. At the top of the list is the most highly evolved, Sol, and at the bottom is the lowest evolved, Saturn.

Sol	Gold	The Sun
Luna	Silver	The Moon
Mercury	Mercury	The Star
Venus	Copper	The Star
Jupiter	Tin	The Tower
Mars	Iron	Death
Saturn	Lead	The Hermit

The eight-pointed star symbolizes the eighth sphere of the fixed constellations. This sphere is composed of ether, an eternal, unchanging element, beyond the sphere of the other four. It is the *horos* (boundary) of the pleroma (fullness) of heaven.

Thus, the imagery in the Star shows the spirit has been led through the depths of the unconscious up to the gate of heaven. The dove to the right of Sophia/Aphrodite symbolizes the spirit that is released after descent into the under

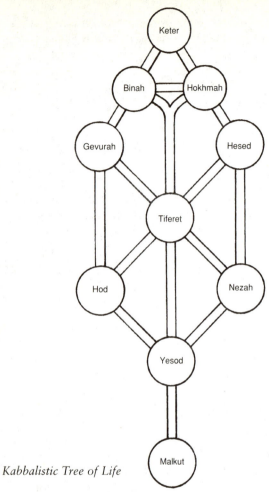

Kabbalistic Tree of Life

world. In classical mythology the dove is a symbol of Aphrodite and Astarte, and in Gnosticism it is a symbol of Sophia. To the ancient Hebrews the dove symbolized Chokmah (Wisdom), or Yahweh's consort or feminine aspect, Shekinah.

The number of the Star, 17, corresponds to the number of Justice, eight (one plus seven equals eight). While Justice's body is the middle pillar of the Tree of Life, the siren's body, with her tails to either side, forms all three pillars. The stream of blood corresponds to the pillar of severity, and the stream of milk to the pillar of mercy. The ten sephirot of the Tree of Life can be positioned on her body, with Keter (crown) at the crown, Binah (understanding) and Hokhmah (wisdom) at the eyes, Gevurah (judgement) and Hesed (mercy) at the breasts, Tiferet (beauty) at the heart, Hod (reverberation) and Nezah (eternity) at the ovaries, Yesod (foundation) at the uterus, and Malkut (kingdom, where the divine manifests in the physical) the birth canal.

Tarot wisdom: The Star represents a secure guide to a higher level of consciousness. It is the Higher Self emerging from the unconscious. The Star indicates a sense of balance and of wellbeing. It can be the peace after a storm, the forgiveness after an argument. It represents the nurturing of the Great Mother: of ourselves, and of others.

XVIII THE MOON

It is not gold unless it is first made silver.
(Rosarium Philosophorum, p. 80)

The Moon represents no alchemical process, but symbolizes the medicine, the white stone, which is a result of the process. The white stone is the culmination of the albedo, or whitening. It is not the philosopher's stone, but is the mother of the stone. What is missing is the masculine seed. The Moon is waiting for her lover brother, the Sun, to join her in the final conjunction that will make the Stone.

The image on this card, inspired by the title page of Michael Maier's *Viatorium*, represents the Moon as one of the premier lunar goddesses, Diana, who is always accompanied by her hounds. Cancer the crab, the moon's native sign, rides in the sky. The dogs represent the passive and active principles: one is dark and sitting, one is light and standing. Diana holds the waxing moon while the waning moon is in the sky, for she rules over all the lunar phases. Her torch relates her to Diana Luciferus, whom the ancient Romans saw as the beacon of the night. She stands at the edge of the waters of the unconscious.

The Moon's number, 18, is a higher aspect of the Great Goddess. It reduces to nine (one plus eight), which in turn is a multiple of three, the symbol of the three aspects of the Goddess.

Tarot wisdom: The Moon represents the night before the dawn. It is a time of patience, rest and reflection, in which the soft energies of the moon compel us to enter the waters of the unconscious, the heart of the mystery.

As the embodiment of the white stone, the Moon represents a level of mastery in which we are in control of our actions, because we are conscious of psychological influences which remain unconscious to others. We have been purified, and now enjoy freedom of choice in our activities and patient acceptance of the activities of others. As it says in the *I Ching*, 'strength is on the inside, and glad acceptance is on the outside.' However, at this level there can be a coldness or flattening of the emotions, because we still need to fully integrate our libido; and so we wait for dawn.

XIX THE SUN

Complexion is of complexion, between two lights, male and female, and then they embrace themselves and couple together, and a perfect light is begotten between them, which there is no light like through all the world.

(Rosarium Philosophorum, p. 36)

With the Sun we reach the third stage of the alchemical opus, the *citrinitas* or yellowing, where the spiritual sun rises to join his lover, the moon. The Sun and Moon are the souls of the Emperor and Empress, and are here joined in the second or greater conjunction, the *hieros gamos*, or sacred marriage.

The Lovers have integrated their shadow, the Devil. As Sol and Luna, they are joined under one crown, the symbol of domination and mastery. They have reached the goal of the Work. The circle with a dot in the middle is the alchemical symbol for gold, and is also the hieroglyph for Ra (*hru*), the Egyptian sun god, whose names means 'sun' or 'day'. Indeed, a new day is dawning. The image on this card is inspired by the title page of *Le Voyage des Princes Fortunez*, (*The Journey of the Fortunate Princes*), 1610.

This second conjunction represented by the Sun is also called multiplication, or the production of the philosopher's stone. The alchemist reaps what he has sown. The operation is performed by the Stone itself, not by the alchemist, who allows it to happen. Essentially, the substance has been killed and burned in the earth, and now is reborn and multiplies like grain. The power of projection is multiplied to infinity, beyond time. In the mystery of Osiris, the Egyptian god of the underworld (and so of death and rebirth), grains of barley were placed on a coffin. When the grains sprouted, Osiris was said to have arisen.

The number of the Sun, 19, is unity. It refers back to the initial unity of all things, the Monad, represented by the number one (one plus nine equals 10, which in turn reduces to one.) The Sun marks a complete revolution on the Wheel of Fortune.

Tarot wisdom: The dawn, or the aurora, is a state of radiant health and wellbeing. We are cleansed of the past as we bask in the healing rays of the new sun. This sun is the internal illumination that previously we were too blind to see; it dawns when we bring our masculine and feminine sides into unity and balance. In Jungian terms this is when our anima or animus joins our conscious mind – represented by a figure of our own sex. It is also the ripening of the white stone as it is reddened by the fire of our libido, the Devil. When all four aspects of our personality – feminine, masculine, persona and shadow – are integrated, we can experience the Higher Self, which is both our centre and our collective whole.

In this state we are motivated and inspired by our desires, but have the maturity to see the yearnings of our soul that are at their root. We have gained the patience to remain unattached to the goal of our quest, manipulating no one and having the strength to simply do what is called for in the present.

XX JUDGEMENT

Awaken from Hades! Arise from the tomb and rouse thyself from darkness! For thou hast clothed thyself with spirituality and divinity, since the voice of the resurrection has sounded and the medicine of life has entered into thee.

(Archelaos, in Alchemy, by E.J. Holmyard, p. 31)

After the *hieros gamos* of the Sun, the white stone yellows, and then begins to redden and mature. Its power has increased. Judgement refers to the stone's ability to heal and rejuvenate, symbolized here by the bodies of the dead Lovers rising from their graves. Like a scene from the final judgement, Gabriel summons them to rejoin their souls, Sol and Luna, who are existing on a higher plane, one with the light of the inner sun.

The image on this card, inspired by Michael Meier's *Tripus aureus* (1618), depicts the alchemical process called the reviving or resurrection, in which the matter of the work which was killed in the nigredo is revived by the power of the stone. This is demonstrated by the stone's ability to transmute base metals into gold. To the alchemist base metals are dead, and become resurrected by becoming gold, the highest degree of their perfection. The central symbol, the grain sprouting from the skull, is a reference to the agricultural mysteries of Ancient Egypt (*see The Sun card*). In the centre of the *ouroboros* of time, the place of immortality, life emerges from death; the grain, like Osiris, or Christ, is reborn from the earth.

The number of Judgement is 20, which reduces to two, the number of the High Priestess, guardian of the feminine mysteries. The two parts, spirit and body, are reunited in the soul. The rebirthing, from the womb of the earth, is guided by the Great Goddess.

Tarot wisdom: Judgement is a time of rejuvenation and healing. To accomplish this we must let go of what is dead or meaningless in our lives. It is a time to look at our behaviour and review our past, and to right wrongs that we have done before they come back to haunt us. Our future judgement must be based on the truth of our experiences.

XXI THE WORLD

Long life and health are in her right hand and glory and immense riches in her left. Her ways are beautiful and praiseworthy works and neither despicable nor bad, and her paths are measured and not hasty, but connected with persistent continuous hard work. She is the tree of life for everybody who understands her and a light which is never extinguished.

(Aurora Consurgens, in *Alchemy* by von Franz p. 187)*

The World brings us to the culmination of the Great Work. Alchemically, the world is the final red stage, the rubedo, in which the red stone of the philosophers is formed. The stone, symbolized by the heart, is composed of pure spiritual essence, the heart or soul of the world (Anima Mundi), which is personified as the nude woman in the centre. In alchemy the Great Work is called the work of the woman. In Renaissance art nudity represents truth.

In the Tarot of Marseilles the World is represented by a female nude surrounded by a wreath, and with symbols of the four evangelists in the corners. These symbols – the winged lion, bull, eagle and man – are commonly associated with the four elements through their connection with the four fixed signs of the zodiac – Leo, Taurus, Scorpio and Aquarius. Therefore, the figure in the centre of this quincunx could easily be interpreted as representing the *quinta essentia*, the element that unifies the other four. This card provides the best evidence that the Tarot expresses an alchemical, Neoplatonic philosophy, and not orthodox Christian thought.

Our alchemical World stands in the centre of the *ouroboros* of time, which forms a wreath around her, signifying that she is beyond time and yet is all time at once, and thus the source of immortality.

She is the other half of Hermes, his inner soul (anima). She holds his caduceus and wears his winged sandals. The caduceus has blossomed wings and has evolved from the green of the Magician (the *prima materia*) to gold. It symbolizes the power of the stone to heal any illness, to change base metal into gold. The stone is also an elixir of life and is shown as a liquid or medicine in the form of the red drop at the bottom of the card. It is life-giving and perfecting. The rose on top symbolizes the perfection of the Work. It has five petals symbolizing the invisible *quinta essentia*, which holds the elements in unison. The World expresses the feminine essence of divinity that we can perceive and underlies all matter.

The number of the World, 21, reduces to three (two plus one equals three), the first complete number, and the number of the Empress, the ruler of the physical world. Twenty-one is the completion of everything – the Anima Mundi revealed. Though numbered 21, the World is really the twenty-second card in the Major Arcana, since the first card, the Fool, is numbered zero. In numerology twenty-two is considered a master number, the number of the Great Architect and of the angelic kingdom.

Tarot wisdom: The World is the achievement and culmination of our goals. On the highest level it is the merging of our individual personality with the Anima Mundi, the soul of the world. The Anima Mundi strains the ability of words to describe it, and it can seem paradoxical. To the Neoplatonic philosopher it is the highest form of the divine presence that we can comprehend. It is at the centre and the circumference of being. It is outside space and time, and yet here now. It is composed of neither matter nor energy, but is the mother of both, continually creating the universe. It is the intelligent, compassionate guide that is evident in the evolution of life. It is both masculine and feminine. Though dual-sexed, we call it 'she'.

The Anima Mundi has been with us guiding us throughout the journey; we could not be alive unless this was so. She was with us when we were the Fool in the beginning. We are still that same fool now; the only difference is that we have dropped our blindfold and have become conscious of her for the first time. Now we are aware of the infinite creative potential that was here all the time. This knowledge is bliss.

> This stone is had in small regard
> With men of slender wit
> But yet the wise and learned sort
> Make great account of it.
> (*Rosarium Philosophorum*, p. 11)

4

THE MINOR ARCANA

T HE Minor Arcana of the Alchemical Tarot is composed of four suits – coins, vessels, swords and staffs – each of which has 10 pip cards and four court cards. Each suit, number and court person has its own associations and symbolic meanings, and these are summarized below. In addition, each card bears a different alchemical image, thus adding depth to the interpretations possible. In the Alchemical Tarot coins are comparable to the pentacles suit of the Rider–Waite deck, and vessels to cups. In the court cards a lady has replaced the page.

Suits

Coins: The material world, acquisitions of wealth and possessions; our connection to the Earth and Nature; sensation; matters pertaining to the physical plane; the element of earth.

Vessels: Emotions, love, pleasures in life; matters pertaining to the unconscious, intuition and inner planes; the element of water.

Swords: Reason, thought, logic, will, courage, verbal skill; matters pertaining to the mind and survival in the world; the element of air.

Staffs: Inspiration, energy, passion, feeling, enterprise, ambition; matters pertaining to the 'spark of life'; the element of fire.

Numbers

Ace: Beginnings; start of something new
Two: Formation, polarity; coming together of opposites
Three: Growth, energy, creativity, fertilization
Four: Practical attainment, the physical plane, stability
Five: Change; upset in equilibrium; spirit
Six: Harmony, love
Seven: Hero's journey; development of soul; facing complex choices; evolution
Eight: Setting priorities and goals; practicality; balance
Nine: Attainment, bringing things to an end; completion
Ten: The end result of a phase or cycle; beginning again; the many returning to the one

Court Cards

Lady: Youthful innocence, grace; art
Knight: Protection, strength, ambition; questing
Queen: Awareness, nurturing; the power to choose
King: Control, discipline, resolve; mastery

Here are descriptions and explanations of each card in the Minor Arcana, which will assist you in your work with the Alchemical Tarot:

ACE OF COINS

A rabbit is in front of a large coin nestled in front of a bower of the earth. The coin shows the four directions or elements radiating from a diamond-shaped hole. The hole in the centre is the *quinta essentia*, the womb-like space that allows the creation of physical matter. This card, which introduces the suit associated with the element earth, shows how the matter emanates from and encases the soul.

Tarot wisdom: You are at the beginning of wellbeing, which could pertain to physical health, material comfort, or receiving or giving nurturing. You are on the right path to acquisitions, wealth and success in the material world. Do not forget, however, that every manifestation in the material world emanates from the spirit.

TWO OF COINS

The image on the card shows an alchemical lemniscate surrounding a sun and moon; these are in the form of a gold solar coin and a silver lunar coin, representing the masculine and feminine. In the Renaissance the two of coins was an important card because it bore the name of the deck's publisher on a banner shaped like this lemniscate.

The lemniscate is crowned by two animal heads. The lion represents the fixed in alchemy; here it swallows the eagle, which is volatile. This is a fitting image for the earth suit, for it shows fixation in the material plane. A certain danger is present because of the polarization of the masculine and feminine. Their dynamic tension and opposition are being held together in the lemniscate, a manifestation of the Higher Self, which is able to hold these opposites in balance.

Tarot wisdom: You are balancing or holding on to resources. Your wealth will not diminish, though there may be some strains. If you do not have much, the message here is that with economy, much can be accomplished with very few resources. Note that the eagle is really the lion's own tail. Thus, it shows a holding on to what you already have. If the card relates to physical health it means that health is good in spite of stress.

THREE OF COINS

Three coins are attached to a building, representing the alchemical trinity of mercury, salt and sulphur. The building shelters an artist who is at work on a profile.

Tarot wisdom: The card suggests an artist who works for the establishment, or who works at a salaried position. It signifies creativity with security and stability. It also represents bringing the unconscious, in terms of creativity and ideas, into the physical plane. The salt coin, which is over the centre column, denotes stability, for in order to express the unconscious, you need stability in life. The message might relate to receiving patronage or contracts for your creative work, with a minimum risk on your part. The message also could relate to work you have done in the past, or will do in the future, depending on the card's position in a spread.

FOUR OF COINS

A primitively clad man is burying his wealth, his four golden coins, in the ground. Four is the number of the physical, and coins are the suit of the physical. This is a heavily grounded card. It suggests perhaps too much concern for the physical. If it points to imbalance, it indicates a miser. In its more positive aspect it indicates someone who is frugal. Conserving your resources might be wise at times.

Tarot wisdom: You are being overly concerned about physical wellbeing, whether health or wealth. The message suggests that you are holding back on spending money or energy. If things are out of kilter in your life the card appears like a slap on the hand to remind you to regain a more balanced perspective.

FIVE OF COINS

A crippled beggar holds out a hand waiting for alms, unaware that coins – wealth – lie scattered on the ground around him. These four coins bear the symbols of the four elements, while the coin in the sky is the *quinta essentia*, the spiritual element that holds the four elements together. The beggar has overlooked the spirit. No matter how much wealth he acquires, he will not accumulate anything because the *quinta essentia* is missing. The quinta essentia nurtures his self-respect and self-confidence; it allows him to be carefree, generous and creative.

Tarot wisdom: Poverty, ill-health, or loss of self-esteem are present or possible in your life, but the means to turn the situation around are within you. You must open up to the unbounded creative potential of the *quinta essentia*, the world soul, that is at the centre of your being. The same intelligence that continually creates the universe has created you. By accepting the guidance of your higher self you can draw on this power and allow it to transform your life. The acceptance of this higher power leads you into feelings of gratitude, generosity, and freedom from care that are the characteristics of a state of true prosperity. For even if you have an excess of wealth, but have not a generous, carefree spirit, then you are still like this poor beggar.

SIX OF COINS

Two children are playing, and one gives a coin to the other. The coins show ancient symbols for money. Six is the first perfect number; it is the number of Aphrodite and is associated with love. In the suit of coins this card relates to giving love freely.

Tarot wisdom: The card points to generosity, and the innocence of giving without attachment and expectation of return. Children suggest a beginner's mind; that is, being true to your emotions. When you are truly loving, you give innocently. The child with open hands represents accepting. Wisdom will come from the gift, because to accept freely is to love yourself. The owl symbol on the exchanged coin also connotes wisdom. The card may show that in some situations there may be more to the giving than is apparent on the surface. Attachments and expectations may be disguised, but to give or receive without attachment allows wealth to flow freely and keeps one in harmony with the soul of the world. As the *I Ching* states, 'It is the law of heaven to make fullness empty and to make full what is modest; – high mountains are worn down by the waters, and the valleys are filled up.'

SEVEN OF COINS

Seven coins on an obelisk refer to the seven metals in alchemy. They form a ladder of evolution as each is purified and transforms into the one above it. At the top they become gold – perfection – which is shown as the fruit of the tree of life – the philosopher's stone. Seven is the number of completion. It is the hero's number, especially in terms of his tasks. It also represents magic.

Tarot wisdom: The ladder shows the process of evolution, and emphasizes that there is a natural growth order. An end result awaits you because you planted the right seeds and undertook the correct process. You are reaping what you sow. The message also might refer to looking back over your steps, or reviewing your progress. Do not become impatient and try to jump ahead to the end or you will miss crucial steps along the way.

EIGHT OF COINS

A coin-stamper takes blank metal and pounds an image on it. Stacks of coins sit on a rack, every one of them identical. The image suggests work as labour as in factory or repetitive work rather than as creativity. Eight is a higher order of the number four.

Tarot wisdom: You are labouring away to create wealth, but without much creative stimulation. You accumulate money or possessions, and are able to better your circumstances. The message can be either positive or negative, depending on the card's position in a spread.

NINE OF COINS

A money tree is full of coins that bear ancient money designs. The coins show a balance of silver and gold, the feminine and masculine principles. Nine is a number of completion.

Tarot wisdom: Nature provides for you. You may reap what you have sown. The message could relate to living off your investments, having more leisure time, or enjoying luxuries. You have life with ease. The card also shows that true health is provided by Nature – the world soul, or the Anima Mundi.

TEN OF COINS

A Renaissance merchant is literally made out of money. He represents someone who is rich and thinks about money a great deal. This person is an entrepreneur, or an opportunist, someone who shrewdly sees the potential for making money in almost any situation. But notice that money covers his eyes, and can also obscure his vision.

Tarot wisdom: You know how to make money, but do not see beyond that. In a negative aspect this could mean being exploitative or self-centred. Remember to keep things in perspective: money is not necessarily wealth, but is a symbol of wealth, a means of exchange for it. The message might also refer to being obsessed with health regimes, perhaps to the point where the regimes themselves are not healthy. Or, it could mean you are well-disciplined about your health habits, because in this situation self-control is called for.

LADY OF COINS

A well-dressed woman with a visibly full purse admires a bouquet of flowers. In the sky is the symbol of Luna, representing the feminine principle.

Tarot wisdom: You are physically or materially well off, and have time to spend in the enjoyment of beauty. This card can also refer to someone who appreciates and admires the physical world, such as a patron of the arts, or a scientist.

KNIGHT OF COINS

An armoured knight stands in a fertile countryside, his castle in the background. He is lean, tall and strong, like a plant with bristly thorns, and his coin bears a protective pentagram. He is a protector of physical wellbeing.

Tarot wisdom: The knight represents someone who guards wealth or health, like an investment banker or a healer. The message could suggest the need to look after your own health or wealth, or to get the advice of an expert who can act as a champion.

QUEEN OF COINS

A crowned nude, like a classical goddess, stands in a garden in front of her castle. In her left arm she holds a cornucopia, a symbol of wealth and the abundance of nature, and in her right hand she holds a coin bearing a six-pointed star drawn with one continuous line, a symbol of balance, harmony and wellbeing.

Tarot wisdom: This card is the personification of health, wealth and wellbeing – a very fortunate state. It can represent our past or present condition, or a goal for the future, depending on its position in the reading.

KING OF COINS

A regal, crowned lion, who is the embodiment of courage and physical strength, holds a coin bearing his own image. He is in a natural setting. He is the essence of satisfaction. His strength and courage are the result of physical balance and harmony with nature. This card relates to the Strength card in the Major Arcana.

Tarot wisdom: The message here is to honour the libido, the animal self, the instincts. Act in strength and possess the courage to pursue what you want. However, keep in mind that wellbeing is best achieved when this is done without attachment to the end result.

ACE OF VESSELS

A fish in water bears on its back a glass vessel containing a heart, from which grows a grape vine. The vessel is the fundamental symbol of femininity, and also represents the alchemist's retort. Here the retort is surrounded by water, the element symbolized by this suit, the symbol of emotions

and the unconscious. The fish, a messenger from the unconscious, is a dweller in water. The heart (a vessel itself) represents a potential philosopher's stone. This transformation
can be brought about through love.

The Ace of Vessels shows that blood (from the heart) is
the water of life. The heart bears fruit in its expression of
love, shown as wine grapes. Wine is a universal symbol for
blood. It is the blood of the vegetable kingdom. Wine is the
blood of Christ in the mystery rite of the Eucharist, a symbol of spiritual rebirth. It is the symbol of the classical vegetation god Dionysus, who expresses the joy and ecstasy of
nature. In alchemy the 'juice of grapes' refers to Mercury,
who, in his role as Good Shepherd, provided a model for
the earliest images of Christ.

Tarot wisdom: You are at a new beginning concerning your
emotions, the unconscious or the soul. The card points out
that both the goal and the source of emotions, represented
by the heart in the vessel, is the need to give and receive
love. Love is the very source of life, and the goal of love is
to be fruitful. Rejoice and release an out-flowing of love,
and allow its returning bounty into your soul, for then the
alchemical vessel of the heart shall sustain new life. If the
message relates to an existing, rather than new, situation it
points to a renewal, a fresh outlook, a 'beginner's mind'.

TWO OF VESSELS

A man and woman are joined as lovers. In the upper vessel
is an Old World rose, which arises from their union. This
rose is also the alchemical rose, a symbol of perfection, like
gold. The polarity expressed in this image is that on the
emotional level there is love and harmony.

Tarot wisdom: There is harmonious, happy love in your
life. The message could pertain to finding a new lover, or

being in harmony with your partner. Together you create balance and stability – a perfect situation. The message also might relate to the inner plane, where a harmony and balance of the masculine and feminine within create perfection for you.

THREE OF VESSELS

Three women are balancing vessels on their heads. They resemble caryatids, which in the Classical world were columns in the shape of women who bear the weight of a building. Like columns, the women here are equal, and are almost identical to each other. On the vessels are symbols for (from left to right) earth, air and fire. The vessel symbolizing water can be found on the head of the Lady of Vessels later in this suit. These women are her companions, her support group. Three women together is suggestive of the Triple Goddess, or of the Three Fates, which is one of the aspects of the Triple Goddess.

Tarot wisdom: Friendship is the central theme here. The message points to a support group. Everyone carries equal weight so that no one person is burdened more than the others. Know that support comes to you when it is needed. The Three Fates suggest either support that has been given in the past, is being given in the present, or might be coming in the future. The fertility aspect of the Triple Goddess might be germane to a reading – like being a supportive midwife at a birth.

FOUR OF VESSELS

An elephant stands on four vessels which act as pillars, and are capable of holding great weight. The image expresses the alchemical axiom of Maria Prophetissa: 'Out of the One comes Two, out of the Two comes Three, and from the Third comes One as the Fourth.' Here, two vessels are the same, the third is slightly different, and the fourth in the set is unique. The card represents physical and emotional balance. The body is in harmony with the emotions. The unconscious is allowed to manifest into the conscious.

Tarot wisdom: In unity there is strength, but it is a delicate balance. You have the inner strength to bear great weight. You will not break under emotional stress and pressure.

FIVE OF VESSELS

Five egg-like vessels were arranged on shelves, but two have fallen. One has broken and has hatched two birds. The birds represent things that were hidden, but are now emerging from the unconscious.

Tarot wisdom: You are experiencing commotion, chaos or a loss, but one that is accompanied by a happy discovery of something unexpected. The message here tells you to look past the loss to what is being gained. Or, it might relate to a sacrifice made or needed to be made in order to gain something better. The message also relates to giving birth, and expresses the labour pains. The birth could be the emergence of an inspiration from the unconscious, perhaps one that seems to happen accidentally, or perhaps one that causes some turmoil in life.

SIX OF VESSELS

A woman fills five vessels by pouring from a sixth; and from one a flower grows. The vessels are of different shapes. From the one vessel she can fill many different ones, each according to its own capacity or needs. The image on the card represents the flowering of love brought through nurturing and tending.

Tarot wisdom: The message reminds you that loving means to nurture and give what is needed. This might relate to personal relationships, or to work. Doing work is in itself an act of love. However, love cannot be forced on someone; true love is to give what is needed to nurture and create strength.

SEVEN OF VESSELS

An alchemical chart shows different-shaped vessels. There is a choice to be made: which one will be selected? Each vessel is suited to a particular task. Only one vessel, the chalice, bears a symbol, and it is of the Anima Mundi, or World Soul.

Tarot wisdom: A choice needs to be made – pick the right tool for the right job, the right path for the journey. When you are faced with a difficult choice, listen to your inner voice; it will guide you to the path that leads to the Anima Mundi. This will be the one that feels right. As the Jungian scholar, Joseph Campbell, said, 'Follow your bliss.'

EIGHT OF VESSELS

A potter uses clay to create vessels by centring them on the wheel. He is totally engrossed in his work, and his vessels are all different. The potter makes an alchemical transformation: he starts with earth, softens it with water, dries it in air, and hardens it with fire. Centred above his wheel is the result of his transformation, a symbol for the Anima Mundi. Eight is the dual aspect of four, and shows here a balance of emotions.

Tarot wisdom: Your work is a creative endeavour, not mere labour. It is engrossing and emotionally satisfying. By immersing yourself in satisfying work, you become centred, and in turn find your centre, which is the Anima Mundi.

NINE OF VESSELS

A sure-footed chamois, which is related to the mountain goat, stands atop an earthen mound and looks out to horizons beyond. The cups can be interpreted to be either in front of the mound, or within it. They are neatly stacked. The image on this card relates to putting your emotional world in order and rising on its support. It is the culmination of emotions.

Tarot wisdom: Take all your emotions and memories, and let bygones be bygones. Be on your way. The emotions and memories associated with the past are your foundation, and can be built upon, but cannot be changed. Do not try to change the past, but look to the future. Do not worry; you are sure footed and will not stumble.

TEN OF VESSELS

An alchemical still is composed of ten vessels united into one piece of apparatus. In ten, the many come back to the one.

Tarot wisdom: No one is emotionally separate and alone. Harmony comes from recognizing your connections to others. Do not isolate yourself – you need others to make your way in life. On a spiritual level recognize your part in the greater whole of the divine cosmos, and know that the function of each individual is essential to the harmony of the whole.

LADY OF VESSELS

A lone, poised woman bears a vessel on her head. She is like a caryatid – a column sculpted like a woman – and stands on the surface of foamy water. She is the feminine embodiment of the suit, an archetype manifested. The lady is at one with the undifferentiated Unus Mundus, but rises above it personified.

Tarot wisdom: You have poise, grace and self-control. Your inner beauty shines out. You have an inner appreciation of how you handle yourself. You are mastering what you have.

KNIGHT OF VESSELS

A knight walks into the water, gathering water in his vessel, and from the blue depths a messenger – the fish – appears. The knight is on a quest for emotional fulfilment. His quest is achieved, and he gets more than he expected in the form of the fish. However, he needs to notice the message. There is also a warning in the image on this card, that if the knight goes in too deep he will not be able to swim with all his armour on.

Tarot wisdom: The message here speaks of the attainment of emotional satisfaction. But, when questing into emotions and the unconscious, do not go off foolishly into the depths. Also, you may be getting a message 'out of the blue', perhaps in the form of a synchronicity. It is an unexpected emotional satisfaction. Maybe you have already received it and, like the knight, need to take notice. Open your eyes to what is around you.

QUEEN OF VESSELS

A mermaid wearing a crown skims the surface of the water with ease, bearing a vessel. She is equally at home in the depths (emotions) or in the air (intellect). Her vessel is sealed – it is a mystery what is inside, and she ponders the mystery. Unlike the Lady of Vessels, who is at one with the Unus Mundus but still separate from it, the Queen of Vessels is completely at one with the Unus Mundus.

Tarot wisdom: You have a mystery to ponder. The unconscious may be trying to present you with something that is yet beyond your grasp. Or perhaps you are only supposed to ponder the mystery. Sometimes to explain the mysteries of life is to diminish them. When a seed is planted in the ground it must remain unseen for a time while it germinates. If we expose it prematurely to the light it will not sprout.

KING OF VESSELS

A whale, the king of the sea, rules over the emotions by recognizing that they are a force of Nature. Thus, he does not try to control the waves but lets them wash over him. He is also an internal source for water, and fills his vessel with his own inner reserves.

Tarot wisdom: To rule your emotions means to let them alone. They are a force of Nature. You are the source of your own satisfaction; do not look to others to provide that for you. Do not allow others to take away your happiness. It is only necessary for you to control your own behaviour, which is independent from the emotions.

ACE OF SWORDS

A basilisk (a serpent with a cock's head) is entwined around a sword, upright in the air, which is its element. A bird is startled by the sight, and hovers, suspended. The sword's hilt ends in a crystal ball, while its guard shows a winged spade, which represents the modern playing card suit sign of spades and the element of air.

In mythology the basilisk is a symbol of wisdom, and is often shown devouring a human. To the Ancients, to be devoured by wisdom was a symbol of enlightenment, or gnosis; it represented initiation into the mysteries. The basilisk is also related to the all-powerful Gnostic god Abraxas, ruler of magic and spiritual powers in the universe, who is portrayed in art as having the head of a cock or lion and the body of a man with legs that terminated in serpents or scorpions. In Christianity the basilisk became a symbol of the Devil. But, as we have learned from alchemy, we have to go through the Devil (darkness) to gain wisdom. The intellect alone is not enough to gain wisdom. Intellect must confront the unconscious, and the two must be integrated. This integration is represented by the basilisk itself.

Tarot wisdom: You are blessed by the beginning of something new in the intellect: an idea, a positive direction, enthusiasm, profound thinking, or originality. The message also relates to the intellectual process that helps to bring creativity and inspiration into the physical plane.

TWO OF SWORDS

Two equal swords are crossed in opposition, challenging one another. Above them hovers Athena's owl, the dual symbol of wisdom and war.

Tarot wisdom: This card represents a debate, a testing of ideas through argument. A challenge to your ideas is in the air. Is it fencing or war? Remember that the goal of a debate is not to dominate your opponent, but to uncover the truth no matter who is right.

THREE OF SWORDS

Three swords enter a heart from the top, their downward thrusting implying negative or destructive aspects. The eye in the centre of the heart symbolizes the soul, and suggests an awakening consciousness. The tears shed by the heart nurture the rose – the goal of alchemy – which grows in a harsh landscape of rocks. The significance of the number three here is the rediscovery of consciousness on a higher level, but it is still incomplete and lacking the dimensionality of the Higher Self. Within the insight gained there is still suffering. However, this suffering is necessary for growth, to achieve the consciousness of the Higher Self.

Tarot wisdom: You are experiencing sorrow, pain and suffering, either emotionally or physically. This card also shows that your own thoughts are behind your suffering, and your disappointments come from your expectations. Remember that pain has a purpose and opens the way to growth. Tears shed are like rain, nurturing something new.

FOUR OF SWORDS

Four downward swords are thrust safely into the earth. Seated either in front – or below within the earth – is a woman, though she is somewhat androgynous in appearance. She is deep in meditation. She has withdrawn into herself. Her unconscious is represented by the earth, which allows the conditions above just to be. She remains unattached to the conditions and to her thoughts, which she releases as they arise.

Tarot wisdom: Take time for meditation, rest, passivity and recouping your strength. Take a break from routine or from stress. This is not a time to take on new challenges, but to restore your resources, both spiritual and physical.

FIVE OF SWORDS

A blacksmith works on a sword. Two broken swords hang on the wall, their points downward, connoting negative forces. Two repaired swords, points up, hang above them, connoting positive forces.

Tarot wisdom: Make the best of a bad situation. Things can be fixed; you can change your life through work, action and positive thinking. The message also points to reclaiming losses. Or, it suggests striking while the iron is hot – there is a right time to take action in every situation.

SIX OF SWORDS

Six swords float horizontally in the air as a ship headed in the same direction skilfully manoeuvres through them, aided by a loving breeze. The image on this card shows that Nature comes to our assistance when we conform to its flow.

Tarot wisdom: You are keeping ahead of troubles with the help of higher forces. These higher forces can manifest themselves through circumstances or people near you. The message also might mean that you should get away from troubles for a while by relaxing, or taking a trip. Or, it may symbolize a safe journey ahead for you.

SEVEN OF SWORDS

A clever fox has been gathering swords to stash away. He comes over a hill with his seventh trophy. Is he building an arsenal for a coming battle? Did he steal the swords from foes, or acquire them openly?

Tarot wisdom: You are completing something, such as bringing a final idea into place or finishing a project. The message also might mean disarming someone, even verbally, while at the same time building up your own resources. Or it may warn of thievery, especially theft of ideas, though sometimes the thief is a hero or a trickster, who heals us by taking negativity from us.

EIGHT OF SWORDS

Eight swords point downwards into the ground to form bars of a cage. A mythical beast with a human-like expression is contained within.

Tarot wisdom: You are holding back the beast within. The beast represents repression, anger, feelings of alienation, or feelings of being cut off from others. It is also inner rage. The human expression on the beast tells that the animal within can be tempered by the Higher Self. When dealing with angry persons, look past the beast and speak to their Higher Selves.

NINE OF SWORDS

Eight swords hang from a ceiling, threatening a man who has but one sword. His way seems open, yet the swords present an emotional threat because he is gripped with fear that they might fall.

Tarot wisdom: You are experiencing needless fear arising from thoughts of impending doom. Negative thinking is creating the fear. There is a way out, however, if you can look past those fears. Or, perhaps you must confront them.

TEN OF SWORDS

A man stabbed with ten swords lies in a pool of blood. An open book lies in the foreground. Ten have come back to one; and negativity has focused on one person.

Tarot wisdom: The worst has happened. Killing criticism, words or even deeds have created physical or emotional pain, or both. The message also expresses the negativity of censorship, which is especially symbolized by the book. The deed is done; now you can heal.

LADY OF SWORDS

A woman sitting on clouds plays a lute and sings. She is the artist of words, poetry and song. A sword hangs in the air above her, and represents the power of her words.

Tarot wisdom: You have eloquence and are at the peak of your verbal or artistic expression. You appreciate the beauty of words and thoughts.

KNIGHT OF SWORDS

A courageous knight with an upraised sword and a lion shield slays a beast. The bones in the foreground suggest that the beast has lived on human flesh. The knight is a hero.

Tarot wisdom: You exhibit positive thinking and bravery, and take action to end your troubles. This card points to decisiveness – you know what you are doing. On the other hand, it might mean you are impetuous, someone who knows only how to confront things head-on, regardless of the wisdom of your deeds. Remember that a hero is measured by the villainy of his foe. The slaying here reminds you that extreme action is only called for in extreme circumstances.

QUEEN OF SWORDS

A winged angel with an armoured crown holds one sword upright sheltered by her red wing. On the other side, under her green wing, she supports a downward-thrust sword. She presents us with a choice between negative thoughts, which are green (unripe, immature), or constructive positive thoughts, which have matured and reddened.

Tarot wisdom: We are the masters of our own destiny. We can bring ourselves down with destructive thinking, or we can create joy and fulfilment in our lives through positive thoughts or affirmations. This direction does not need to be forced, as we gain knowledge we mature, and the positive creative choice becomes natural. This queen can represent someone who has attained that level of maturity, or perhaps she is pointing to positive and negative choices available at this time

KING OF SWORDS

A crowned, royal eagle proudly holds his upraised sword as he stands on the air. He is master of the intellect.

Tarot wisdom: You have a deep-seated inner confidence. This is true inner strength that does not have to be displayed. Your communication is clear and decisive; you are not afraid to speak your mind. You are capable of choosing whether or not to respond to the prompts of others, and to separate false preconceptions from fact.

ACE OF STAFFS

A burning staff is in the midst of its element, fire. It stands with a living leaf, suggesting the club suit of modern playing cards. At the base of the staff is the mythical animal of fire, the salamander.

The salamander is an interesting creature in world mythology and folklore. Real salamanders are small, lizard-like amphibians that live in moist places. The mythical salamander was, in ancient times, believed to be poisonous and also able to survive fire.

Pliny said that the salamander 'seeks the hottest fire to breed in, but quenches it with the extreme frigidity of its body'. In alchemy the salamander was one symbol of the *prima materia*. In the alchemical process it plays the role of helping the substance under transformation to give up its secret fire. This fire will help the philosopher's stone claim its final power.

As the salamander lives in the fire so does the stone.
(*Alalanta Fugiens*, in *The Golden Game*, p. 101)

In the Ace of Staffs, a card of beginnings, the salamander signifies primal energies and transformative powers.

Tarot wisdom: You are experiencing the beginning or birth of something that will require a lot of energy, like a new job, a new project or a new relationship. Even though it requires energy, it gives energy back to you in reward.

TWO OF STAFFS

A hand holding a staff emerges from a cloud and lights the end of its staff from an already burning staff planted in the ground. At the base of the grounded torch is the symbol for Venus; above the hand in the air is the symbol for Mercury, which suggests the uniting of lovers. Fertility is suggested by the flowers around the grounded staff. There is life springing from this union.

Tarot wisdom: Like begets like; and one torch lights another. Your enthusiasm is contagious. The small branch on the grounded, feminine staff that is aflame represents the offspring of the union. Whether the offspring is a child or a result of work this will take on a life of its own. Alchemically this card represents the seed of three, which is contained in two. Or, the small flaming branch might represent something which has its own energy and chooses not to join in the union.

THREE OF STAFFS

Two staffs on a shore await an oncoming ship with a burning mast. The fire is contained and the ship is not threatened. An eye is painted on the bow to guide the ship, a custom that has been common in the Mediterranean since ancient times.

Tarot wisdom: Your ship has come in. Energy has been spent, and now it returns in reward. What you have been waiting for is arriving; the project will be complete. Or, the message may point to the arrival of reinforcements to help out in a tough situation.

FOUR OF STAFFS

A man and woman make a commitment to one another in a marriage ceremony that takes place within a sacred space created by four burning staffs.

Tarot wisdom: Fire is energy, in this case the energy of love and passion. Four is the number of physical manifestation. This card depicts a structured and enduring passion. It could refer to a marriage, a partnership or another relationship that is meant to endure.

FIVE OF STAFFS

A hand's fingers are transformed into burning staffs. Five is the number of creativity; this is the creative hand of an artist, inventor, scientist or entrepreneur. The fire is the energy and enthusiasm directed into the project – but will the fire consume the hand, and thus the life energy of the creator? This will not happen if the hand is a channel for energy from a higher force.

Tarot wisdom: You are enthusiastic and inspired by your work or other fires (channels for your energy). Your creative energy is at its peak, fuelled by the spirit. If your work is all-consuming, or if you are not in touch with your higher self, the message warns that you risk burning yourself up. Do not become a workaholic.

SIX OF STAFFS

An artisan, wearing a worker's apron, is being honoured. He stands on a cloud and wears a laurel wreath. Under his feet are the alchemical symbols for silver and gold. Many torches are held up in his honour, but we can only see the arms of the individuals holding them, and they remain anonymous. When we compare their size to that of the artisan, they seem gigantic, almost threatening.

Tarot wisdom: You receive love in the form of respect and admiration. The success of your project has made you an example for others. This is your moment of glory. However, from the cloud it is a long way down; do not become complacent or rest on your laurels. Fame has its negative side, too.

SEVEN OF STAFFS

Two dogs fight and one bites the other on the face. In the background seven staffs form a gnarled tangle that has a menacing appearance.

Tarot wisdom: This is a dog-eat-dog world. You meet competition from others or are engaged in a struggle for superiority. This message speaks to the negative aspects of competition, where people try to win by causing others to lose.

EIGHT OF STAFFS

A workman diligently chops back staffs to get them in balance. Perhaps he will be practical and use the cut wood.

Tarot wisdom: You can achieve a better balance in your life by trimming and cutting back. Do not try to take on too much work. Re-evaluate, assess what is important and what is expendable, and use your energy wisely. The message also suggests prudence and practicality. The worker in the image on this card can use what he cuts to build a fire. Is there a situation in your life where you can act similarly? Or the message may address taking care of an emergency – for example, trees are cut to stop a forest fire from spreading.

NINE OF STAFFS

A wolf is sacrificed in a fire. This is an alchemical symbol representing the restoration of the king, who was devoured by the wolf.

Tarot wisdom: You face a calamity; a fire is out of hand. Fire consumes you to the point of exhaustion or illness. The message also suggests sacrifice, especially for a higher purpose, like suffering for the good of others, or being a martyr, or subduing the animal passions for spiritual purpose.

TEN OF STAFFS

A phoenix, also called the firebird, rises from a fire of ten staffs. In mythology the phoenix is the classic symbol of sacrifice by death so that rebirth can take place. This creature immolates itself and is burnt in the fire. After three days, it rises anew from the ashes. The phoenix is also a solar symbol, representing the cycle of the sun as it is born again every day. In alchemy the phoenix is a symbol for the philosopher's stone, the consummation of the Work. In psychology the phoenix represents the birth of a new personality.

Tarot wisdom: You have been transformed by your experiences. You have been tested by fire; your old self has died away, and a new self is being born. You are renewed.

LADY OF STAFFS

A woman in Classical dress stands in a desert landscape and holds a burning staff. Looking upon it with admiration, she begins to dance.

Tarot wisdom: You are fascinated by light and energy, and have a sense of appreciation and wonder. You have mastered the art of graceful movement in all ways. You are well suited to start an endeavour in a new area, to make the desert bloom.

KNIGHT OF STAFFS

A knight stands in a desert landscape holding a burning staff. His helmet bears red, fire-like plumes

Tarot wisdom: You enjoy health and vitality. You are ready to create something new, or take on challenges in a new area. Your stamina is an inspiration to others.

QUEEN OF STAFFS

A crowned woman in Classical dress stands in the desert holding two torches. The torch in her left hand is raw and natural, left as it was when taken from a tree. The other torch is refined, and has been carved in a decorative Classical design.

Tarot wisdom: Like the Queen of Swords, the Queen of Staffs is presenting us with a choice. In this case it is between that which is natural, unprocessed, or possibly crude, and that which is refined or sophisticated. For more insight into these choices look at the cards that flank this one in your layout.

KING OF STAFFS

A scaly-winged dragon coils around the base of a flaming staff. His crown is formed naturally by his scales; he has crowned himself.

Tarot wisdom: Our primitive animal passions are the source of our life energy. They must not be vilified. The dragon coiled around the staff is synonymous with the Tantric kundalini force, a serpent-like energy which coils at the base of the spine and is the source of psychic power. This is a card of inner strength; it tells us that we have energy in reserve.

5

ALCHEMICAL SPREADS
AND MEDITATIONS

CARL G. Jung once observed that to get in touch with the self is to find the centre. The centre is everywhere – it is the all-pervasive Anima Mundi, which in the Tarot is represented by the World card. Jung's student and colleague, Marie-Louise von Franz, states that getting in touch with the Anima Mundi leads to healing and a sense of being nurtured. She observes that the primary technique for us to reach the Anima Mundi is divination.

The basis of all divinatory, or mantic, arts is to create a random or chaotic pattern and examine it for meaning. The pattern represents the essence of the moment – rather like the way a photograph preserves a scene or expression.

The patterns in mantic arts are not considered to be truly random or haphazard, but the product of divine will, or the flow of the universe. For example, the Gnostics believed that making decisions by choosing lots was to discover the choice of God.

Tarot spreads can be seen as expressions of the divine order of the cosmos, and show a person's place in that order at the moment of a reading. The spreads function like a net, or numbered grid, which captures the random pattern of archetypes and reveals their significance to an individual.

Spreads

The spreads here are offered to help you get started in using the Alchemical Tarot. With practice, however, you will soon have new ideas for making your own spreads. Just keep in mind the idea of the grid, and assign a meaning to each card position on it. Make use of the mystical meaning of numbers in designing your spreads: think about the total number of cards in a spread, and the number of cards in lines and patterns.

The number three appears repeatedly in the spreads in this chapter. The energy of three is creative power, indicating forward movement, and totality. It is the first complete number. Because it has three dimensions it is capable of describing physical reality, and because time has a past, a present and a future, the number three can tell a story.

Some of these spreads specifically call for three advice cards as part of the pattern. In fact, any spread can be crowned with three advice cards for the querent whenever additional information or insight needs to be sought. When the advice cards are an addition to a spread and not part of the basic pattern, shuffle the cards again before selecting them.

Reading the Tarot requires a similar approach to interpreting a dream. The trick to providing a good reading is to see what is going on within the pictures, and how the pictures in a spread relate to each other and to the querent. For this reason you will find it useful to study dream interpretation, mythology and symbolism to help augment your work with the Tarot. It is also helpful to be familiar with the description of each card in the book; however, interpretations in the book should be considered as guidelines, not the final word.

While you have a great deal of latitude in reading spreads, keep in mind that there is a basic framework.

The idea of predicting the future may seem illogical, or even frightening to some people, so to dispel any negative associations let us clarify what this means. Each of us is actually creating our future by our thoughts and actions in the present. We participate in this creation consciously but it tends to be guided by our unconscious mind. The cards enable us to communicate with the unconscious and can therefore show us where we are headed. This destination is not an irreversible fate, however. If the querent does not like where he or she is headed then the reading can help to change or at least modify that direction. This is the only valid reason to ask for a prediction, so be sure to also ask for advice.

Let the querent cut the cards once with his or her left hand (symbolizing intuition) while stating the purpose of the reading – it should be specific. Then take the cards and shuffle them loosely, stopping when you feel the intuition to cease. Let the querent cut – again with the left hand – by removing a block of cards from the top of the deck and setting it aside. Lay the next three cards out in a line from left to right.

Now look at the cards as one picture, and interpret it as you would a dream. It will be helpful to notice in what direction the characters are facing. The cards could show a story which begins on the left and ends on the right, or the action could start on the right and proceed in the opposite direction. Perhaps the central figure is dominant – looking directly at you. In this case it could be offering you a choice, represented by the cards on either side of it, or it could be balancing these forces. Use your intuition.

The Alchemical Celtic Cross

Of all Tarot spreads the Celtic Cross is the most popular, and is one of the best for divination, as it shows many facets – past, present and future – of any given situation.

Trump cards are archetypal forces. Pip and court cards describe the mundane world of the four elements:

Staffs – fire – energy, work, passion, feeling
Swords – air – ideas, words, thinking
Vessels – water – emotions, the unconscious, intuition
Coins – earth – physical wellbeing, health, wealth, sensation

Once you are comfortable with the spreads described here, experiment by making your own variations. Spreads can be adapted to suit any reading. When you tune in to the Anima Mundi you will be guided by intuition and inspiration to see spreads and readings in novel ways.

Here are some time-tested spreads which are especially effective with the Alchemical Tarot. These layouts allow for fluidity in interpretation, and so help you to use your intuition. The placements and their meanings are not to be followed rigidly, but are general guidelines.

The Story

This is probably the simplest spread you will ever find, but it is nonetheless a powerful one. It uses three Tarot cards and you read the three images as one picture, a story. Every story – or situation – has a beginning, a middle and an end, making a total of three parts.

To start, make sure that none of the cards in the deck is upside down in relation to the others. This will make it easier to place the cards right side up in your reading. This is recommended for all readings because it allows the pictures to communicate more clearly.

Next, the querent must decide the purpose of the reading. The purpose can be a clarification of a past or present situation, advice, the possible outcome of a course of action, or a prediction of the future.

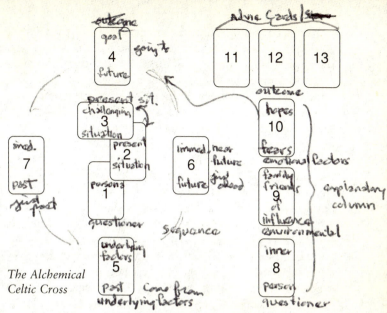

The Alchemical Celtic Cross

Traditionally, the Celtic Cross is made with ten cards plus a significator, which is the card the querent chooses to represent himself or herself in the reading.

The Alchemical Celtic Cross is made with 13 cards. The alchemical vibration of 13 makes it a power number: one plus three equals four, the number of solidity and wholeness. Thirteen is an aspect of four; it is not quite the wholeness, but a striving towards it. The purpose of a reading is a striving towards balance and wholeness in life.

Thirteen is also considered by many to be a lucky number, not an unlucky one, because of its associations with the moon, and therefore the Goddess. There are 13 lunar cycles in a calendar year. The Goddess rules the moon, which governs the unconscious, emotions, intuition and creativity. In a good reading intuition runs high, and the reader gains access to the unconscious to find hidden factors concerning the reading.

Start as before, letting the querent cut the cards while stating the purpose of the reading. Then, let the cards themselves pick the significator. Shuffle and let the querent draw one randomly from the pack, and place it down. This card, number one, represents the persona of the querent – the personality that he or she displays to the outside world.

Shuffle again, and let the querent remove the top block as before. Starting with the top card, lay them out in the order shown in the diagram. Card number two, in the centre of the equilateral cross, represents the present situation. Across it place the third card, which is the challenging situation (this card can be placed on its side with its head to your right). The next four cards build the time sequence. Card number four, at the crown, represents the future, the goal. Card number five, at the bottom, represents the past, the underlying factors that have created or influenced the present situation and the challenge. To the right place card number six, which represents the immediate future. To the left place card number seven, which represents the immediate past. Then move on to the explanatory column to the right.

At the base of the column, card number eight represents the inner person. Moving up the column, card number nine represents the family and friends who are most influential in the situation. Card number 10 represents the querent's hopes and fears. Pay attention to this card, for it is in turn related to card number four, the goal. At the top of the column, place three cards in a line, using the significator card and your intuition to guide you as to the order, from left to right or from right to left. These are the advice cards, and, like the three cards in the Story spread, should be read as a whole picture.

Then go through the cards in order, reading it as you would a story. Interpret the explanatory column, using the time sequence cards as guides. Look at the direction the cards face to intuit the influences. Cards that face your left represent factors focused on the past, fading into the past, or with an inability to move forwards. Cards facing right indicate new events coming into being, focused on the as-yet unmanifest future, or with forward movement and progress. Notice how the cards relate to each other. Are some pointing at others? Are they facing each other, or is one turning its back on another?

The Relationship Triangle

This spread is good for assessing relationships between the querent and another person, and for seeing their interactions and underlying attitudes towards each other and the relationship. We have our old friend the number three again, bringing creativity and forward movement to the reading. The vibration of three is beneficial to relationships that have stalled or are clouded by uncertainties. The Relationship Triangle can be applied to relationships between two persons, or between a person and a job, home, culture, city or other environment. The Anima Mundi is broad, and we can focus in on whatever part of it we desire through the cards.

The cards are laid out in three groups of three. You can work in either direction, left to right or right to left, to lay them out. Start by letting the querent cut as before.

The Relationship Triangle

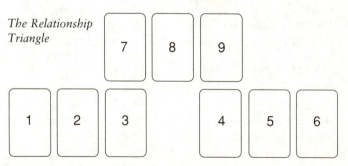

On the left, lay out the first line of three cards. This line represents the querent. Skip a space, and on the right lay out the second line of three cards, which represents the other half of the relationship – person, place, job, etc. On top, place the third line of three cards, which represents the relationship itself, and reveals the dynamics at work. Use the Story spread approach to read each line of three as a whole picture. Then look at all three lines to give a complete reading.

The Situation Pyramid

This reading gives a picture of where the querent sits in any situation. It is good for providing insights into circumstances and the forces in motion.

The cards are laid out in a pyramid shape. Three cards form the bottom and represent the foundation of the situation. The second line of two cards represents events that more recently underlie the present. A single card at the top is the situation itself.

The Journey of Life

The Journey of Life spread shows where a querent stands along life's path.

Lay out seven cards in an arc, moving from right to left. The arc represents a part of the querent's life journey. The future lies on the right, the past lies on the left. The querent is somewhere in between. Read the cards as a story of the querent's life, and his or her position along the journey.

The Alchemical Ladder

The equation of seven metals with the seven planets of the Ancients is basic to alchemy. The Ancients believed that the soul went through a planetary ladder after death, which was a purification process (*see The Star in Chapter 3*). The alchemists related each planet to a metal, which also formed a mystical ladder as each metal evolved into its purer essence in the alchemical process. Both of these ladders correspond on a spiritual plane to the seven energy zones in the body commonly called by their Hindu name, chakras, but which are known in many traditions.

In Hindu and Buddhist yogas, chakras (from the Sanskrit for 'wheels') are vortexes which penetrate the body and the body's aura, through which various energies, including the universal life force, are received, transformed and distributed. The chakras are related to seven zones or sections of the body that each rule over different emotions and personality traits. They play a vital role in physical, mental and emotional health and in spiritual development. They are invisible to ordinary sight but may be perceived by clairvoyance.

This reading can give a picture of the present condition of these energy zones in the querent. Since few people have achieved a perfect balance of energy in all these zones, it can be helpful in depicting strengths and weaknesses in the querent's personality, and in uncovering energy blocks which may underlie illness. When exposing a weakness or illness be sure to ask the cards for advice on how to work towards balance and health – this is the only compelling reason for carrying out this reading.

The Alchemical Ladder relates the seven metals and planets of alchemy to the energy zones. Lay out seven cards in a vertical line from bottom to top. Interpret each one using the guidelines that follow and basing your reading on the function of the zone, the symbolic and alchemical meanings of the corresponding metal and planet, and the Tarot card.

Zone	Metal	Planet
Root	Lead	Saturn
Sacral	Iron	Mars
Solar plexus	Tin	Jupiter
Hear	Copper	Venus
Throat	Mercury	Mercury
Brow (third eye)	Silver	Moon
Crown	Gold	Sun

Card 1

Zone: Root. Located at the base of the spine, this zone is concerned with self-preservation, your animal nature and the physical senses; that is, the basic elements of life. When activated, it gives a feeling of wellbeing and security. It can make a person feel solid and grounded. When blocked, it produces insecurity and a lack of control over your life.

Metal: Lead. The *prima materia* of all metals, without which the alchemical process cannot begin. Lead, the heaviest of the alchemical metals, is the beginning of the Opus, the nigredo stage.

Planet: Saturn. Heavy, slow, profound and sombre, this planet rules time, and is often portrayed as an old man with a scythe and hourglass. Its dark demeanour corresponds to the nigredo of alchemy.

Card 2

Zone: Sacral. This zone is the area where the genitals are located, and it governs sexuality and reproduction. It gives you a sense of joy and humour, besides sexual desire. When blocked, it creates anger, fear and frustration.

Metal: Iron. A metal of secondary importance in alchemy, iron represents strength, especially of a vital, physical nature. The Ancient Greeks drank tonics of rusted iron in wine to relieve exhaustion.

Planet: Mars. This red-tinged planet is associated with strength, aggression, virility and sexuality.

Card 3

Zone: Solar plexus. Located just above the navel, this zone is associated with hunger and wants. It is the point where astral energy enters an individual's aura. It affects the adrenals, pancreas, liver and stomach. When activated it yields assertiveness and initiative. When blocked, it creates laziness, fear, procrastination and loss of privacy.

Metal: Tin. A metal of lesser importance in alchemy, tin was known to the Ancient Egyptians and Phoenicians, and was once more highly valued than copper because its addition to copper created the alloy bronze. At one time it was also used to treat fevers and hysteria.

Planet: Jupiter. The Babylonians and Ancient Greeks called Jupiter the 'sun of the night'. They associated it with wisdom and power (use of the intuition or 'gut' instincts), but also with mystery and remoteness.

Card 4

Zone: Heart. Located in the centre of the chest, the heart governs the thymus gland and influences immunity to disease. It is linked to higher consciousness, love, compassion and a love of beauty. When blocked, it is linked to emotional suffering and pain.

Metal: Copper. A secondary metal in alchemy, copper is of great practicality, malleability and beauty.

Planet: Venus. This planet represents beauty, love, ease, pleasure and brightness.

Card 5

Zone: Throat. This zone is associated with creativity and self-expression, and the search for truth. It is prominent in musicians, singers, composers, artists and public speakers. It also influences the thyroid and parathyroid glands, and metabolism. When blocked, it can create inhibitions, the inability to speak one's mind and a lack of appreciation.

Metal: Mercury. An important alchemical symbol of transformation, and of the *prima materia*. The actual liquid metal inspired this association because it was obtained by roasting the red stone, cinnabar, prized for its ability to extract gold from its matrix, and essential to the process of gilding.

Planet: Mercury. The planet closest to the sun is quick and elusive, and is associated with good communication skills, a brilliant imagination, and a facile mind.

Card 6

Zone: Brow. Located between the brows, this zone is called the 'third eye' because of its influence over psychic sense and spiritual enlightenment. The brow is associated with the pituitary gland, the pineal gland, intelligence, intuition and psychic powers. It is related to intelligence and reason. When blocked, it can make one feel confused and slow at solving problems.

Metal: Silver. A precious metal, and one of the desired objects of the alchemists. The Ancients used silver as a remedy for all disorders affecting the brain.

Planet: Luna. The moon, personified by the Goddess, rules the rhythms of life, the unconscious and the hidden mysteries.

Card 7

Zone: Crown. Located at the top of the head, this zone is not associated with any glands, but reveals the individual's level of conscious evolution. In yoga it is believed that the crown chakra cannot be activated until all the other chakras are refined and balanced. Then, it brings supreme enlightenment and cosmic consciousness. Others believe that it always has an affect on the personality, that it gives a sense of perspective and awareness. When blocked, you can become caught up in personal concerns.

Metal: Gold. The most precious of all metals, universally revered as a magical and otherworldly metal. Gold was the desired goal of alchemists, and could only be obtained after a precise alchemical process was followed. Gold was once believed to purify the blood.

Planet: Sol. The sun represents the light of spiritual consciousness, the all-seeing eye that comprehends the oneness of mystical enlightenment.

Meditations

Not all alchemy goes on in a physical laboratory. The highest alchemy takes place in the laboratory of the soul, and since ancient times meditations have been part of alchemy.

The Gnostic alchemist Zosimos (*circa* AD 330), called the father of the Hellenistic alchemical tradition, wrote that 'genuine' alchemical transformations occur when the alchemist's soul unites with the divine spirit (nous), which orders the universe. This unison can be brought about through meditation, Zosimos said. Similarly, Gerard Dorn (1560s–80s), a student of Paracelsus, recommended a meditation that would open the *fenestrae aeternitatis*, the 'window into eternity'. In this meditation the alchemist was to subdue the instinctual body by separating from it the soul and spirit. The soul and spirit were to be fused together, and then reunited with a purified body. In psychological terms, this fosters the build-up of a spiritual attitude that enables the alchemist to find his eternal essence – to touch the Unus Mundus.

The use of vivid images, especially allegorical ones, was favoured in Renaissance times as a meditation tool for communing with the divine and for various magical operations on higher planes of consciousness. It was in the late nineteenth century, however, that meditational images found greater significance. In particular, the Hermetic Order of the Golden Dawn saw Tarot images as a powerful way to access the astral byways in occult training. The poet William Butler Yeats, who joined the Golden Dawn in 1890, was intrigued by the Tarot. He believed he had experienced the One through the Anima Mundi in meditation.

Contemplation

For this meditation let the Anima Mundi select a card for you. Pick a card at random. What is in it that you need to know, be reminded of, develop or work with? What the universe hands you may surprise you. Trust the guidance.

Find a room where you will not be disturbed. Choose a comfortable place where you can sit with your back straight and upright. This can be the floor – a firm pillow is helpful – or a chair that does not cause you to slouch.

At first pay attention solely to your breath until you find

yourself breathing deeply and rhythmically from your abdomen. In this relaxed state, take the card and place it in front of you in a way that makes it easy to gaze on it. Now simply look at it without attaching any thoughts to it. Thoughts will naturally arise, but let go of each one as it comes, watch it drift away, and then return to looking at the card.

This can be done for five to twenty minutes. Throughout the day pay attention to how the image has affected you.

The Opus

This meditation is performed with just the Major Arcana. These cards comprise a powerful group of archetypes that can guide you in a journey of inner growth and alchemical transformation. Starting with the Fool, meditate with each card, one at a time and in order, until you reach the World card. Do not let personal prejudice stop you from using a particular card. All of them have an important message; none of them is either good or bad. When utilized in their numerical order, each card will prepare you for the next.

Starting with the Fool, take the card from the deck and use it for a contemplation meditation. Then keep it with you throughout the day, thinking about it often. Visualize it with your eyes closed; try drawing a picture of it. After doing this for three days the image will become fixed in your mind.

On the third evening take some time to contemplate the card before you go to bed. Then put it beside your bed or under your pillow, and give yourself a verbal suggestion that you will dream about the card that night. In the morning do not rush out of bed, but lay still for a while, and remember the dream. Keep a pad next to the bed so that you can write the dream down, and then interpret the dream.

Proceed this way through the Major Arcana. Do not

rush the process. Take some time to digest what you have experienced.

Active Imagination

The Opus can also be completed in a more advanced form using the technique called active imagination. This method is based on techniques used by the Golden Dawn.

Start as before by contemplating and thinking about the first card for three days. Next, in a quiet room at a time when you are alert and ready to begin, create a safe ritual space by drawing a circle on the floor that is big enough for you to sit in. The circle can be drawn with white string or chalk, or it may just be visualized as white light. Place the four aces, which represent the elements, around the circle so that they are aligned with the four directions. Use your intuition to decide which card is associated with each direction. It is helpful to decide which direction is hot and dry, which is cold and wet, etc.

The circle is a symbol of the Unus Mundus, and when you enter the circle and sit between the four aces, you will complete the form of a quincunx. This will align you with the Anima Mundi, and you will be guided and protected. As you enter the circle, verbally affirm that in this symbol you are one with the Anima Mundi, and that you are safe.

Sit in the circle facing north. Start by contemplating the card until you can hold the image in your mind. Visualize the border of the card as a doorframe, and the coloured rectangle as a painting on the door. Visualize a handle on the door; reach out and grasp the handle, open the door and walk through.

Look around. If you see darkness, look into it and wait – be patient. Feel free to allow yourself to interact with whatever images arise. Allow the experience to come to its natural conclusion. When you have finished you may want to write it down.

Again, perform this meditation with each card in order until you reach the World. Take your time. Alchemy requires patience.

Unus Mundus

This is an advanced meditation to be done after completing the Opus.

In this meditation you begin by laying all 22 of the Major Arcana cards in order on the floor to create a circle. You will create a symbol of the Unus Mundus – a mandala – that incorporates the whole Opus. The Fool will join the World and the Magician together like the head and tail of the *ouroboros*.

Sit in the centre of the circle and contemplate the images of all the cards at once. Visualize how you look in the centre of all those images. Then fix this image in your mind and contemplate it.

This meditation can be performed regularly.

After you have practised meditation exercises with the Alchemical Tarot for a period of time you will undoubtedly notice changes in consciousness. Your dream life especially is likely to be affected; you may have richer, more detailed and archetype-laden dreams. You may also be aware of an improvement in your intuition, inspiration and creativity, as well as in your perception of subtleties in your connection to others and to the Divine.

We wish you well on your personal alchemical journey.

ABOUT THE AUTHORS

Robert M. Place is an award-winning designer, sculptor and painter, who has exhibited his paintings in major New York galleries. He has worked as a commercial artist, designed furniture and is well known for his line of sculptural jewellery which he designs and manufactures with his wife Rose Ann.

Robert received a 1984–5 Crafts Fellowship from the New Jersey State Council on the Arts. He won the 1990 and the 1991 USA national Niche Award for outstanding achievement in sculptural metal. Since 1982 he has continually exhibited his work in group and one-person gallery and museum shows in both America and Europe, including the 1984 and 1988 international Wilhelm Muller Competition in Gmund, Germany, and the 1992 'Wearables' exhibition at the American Craft Museum, New York.

In his designs Robert draws on archetypal symbols found in mythology, religion and alchemy. He feels that his exploration of the relationship between the conscious and the unconscious allows the viewer to participate directly with his work on a non-verbal level.

Recently Robert has begun writing articles and illustrating for books and magazines. *The Alchemical Tarot* is his first book.

For information on Robert's jewellery designs and other products send a stamped self-addressed envelope to:

R. & R. Place
PO Box 541
Saugerties, NY 12477
USA

Rosemary Ellen Guiley is a best-selling and award-winning author of more than 12 books on spirituality, consciousness, human potential and the paranormal. She is a long-time student of alchemy, the Western mysteries, the Tarot, meditation and dreamwork. Her first book on the Tarot, *The Mystical Tarot*, was published by New American Library (1991).

Other books are: *The Miracle of Prayer: True Stories of Blessed Healings* (Pocket Books, 1995); *Angels of Mercy* (Pocket Books, 1994); *Harper's Encyclopedia of Mystical and Paranormal Experience* (HarperCollins, 1991); *The Encyclopedia of Dreams: Symbols and Interpretations* (Crossroad, 1993; Berkeley 1995); *The Atlas of the Mysterious in North America* (Facts On File, 1994); *The Encyclopedia of Ghosts and Spirits* (Facts On File, 1992); *The Encyclopedia of Witches and Witchcraft* (Facts On File, 1989); and *Tales of Reincarnation* (Pocket Books, 1989). In addition she has written two books on vampires in mythology and pop culture.

Rosemary also writes a popular monthly column on consciousness, 'The New Millennium', for *Fate* magazine, and writes articles for various periodicals. She lectures internationally.

For information on her books, audio tapes and lectures/workshops, send a stamped addressed envelope to:

Rosemary Ellen Guiley
1290 Bay Dale Dr.
Arnold
MD 21012
USA

BIBLIOGRAPHY AND RECOMMENDED READING

anonymous. trans. Waite, A. E., The Hermetic Museum (Musaeum Hermeticum), York Beach, Maine, Samuel Weiser Inc., 1990 (originally published Frankfurt, 1612)

anonymous. Ed. McLean, Adam, The Rosary of the Philosophers (Rosarium Philosophorum), London, The Hermetic Trust, 1980

Dummett, Michael, The Visconti–Sforza Tarot Cards, New York, George Braziller Inc., 1986

Gilchrist, Cherry, The Elements of Alchemy, Longmead, Dorset, Element Books, 1991

Giles, Cynthia, The Tarot: History, Mystery and Lore, New York, Paragon House, 1992

Grossinger, Richard, The Alchemical Tradition in the Late Twentieth Century, Berkeley, California, North Atlantic Books, 1979

Guiley, Rosemary Ellen, The Mystical Tarot, New York, New American Library, 1991

Holmyard, E.J., Alchemy, New York, Dover Publications, 1990 (first published 1957)

Jung, Carl G., 'Aion', from The Collected Works of C.G. Jung, vol. 9, part II, Princeton, NJ, Princeton University Press, 1959

—, 'Alchemical Studies', from The Collected Works of C.G. Jung, vol. 13. Princeton, NJ, Princeton University Press, 1967

—, 'The Archetypes of the Collective Unconscious', from The Collected Works of C.G. Jung, vol. 9, part I, Princeton, NJ, Princeton University Press, 1959

—, 'Mysterium Coniunctionis', from The Collected Works of C.G. Jung, vol. 14. Princeton, NJ, Princeton University Press, 1963

—, 'Psychology and Alchemy', 2nd ed. from The Collected Works of C.G. Jung, vol. 12. Princeton, NJ, Princeton University Press, 1953

Kaplan, Stuart R., The Encyclopedia of the Tarot Vol. I, New York, US Games, Inc.,1978

—, The Encyclopedia of the Tarot Vol. II, New York, US Games, Inc., 1986

Klossowski de Rola, Stanislas, The Golden Game: Alchemical Engravings of the Seventeenth Century, New York, George Braziller, Inc., 1988

—, Alchemy: the Secret Art, London, Thames and Hudson, 1973

McLean, Adam, The Alchemical Mandala, Grand Rapid, Mich., Phanes Press, 1989

Moakley, Gertrude, The Tarot Cards Painted by Bonifacio Bembo, New York, The New York Public Library, 1966

O'Neill, Robert, Tarot Symbolism, Lima, Ohio, Fairway Press, 1986

Pollack, Rachel, Seventy-Eight Degrees of Wisdom: A Book of the Tarot; Part I: The Major Arcana, Wellingborough, The Aquarian Press, 1980

—, Seventy-Eight Degrees of Wisdom: A Book of the Tarot; Part II: The Minor Arcana, Wellingborough, The Aquarian Press, 1983

Ruland, Martin, trans. Waite, A. E., A Lexicon of Alchemy, York Beach, Maine, Samule Weiser Inc., 1984 (originally published Frankfurt, 1612)

Stillman, John Maxson, The Story of Alchemy and Early

Chemistry, New York, Dover Publications, 1960 (first published 1924 as The Story of Early Chemistry)

Von Franz, Marie-Louise, Alchemy, Toronto, Inner City Books, 1980

—, Number and Time, Evanston, Ill., Northwestern University Press, 1974

—, On Divination and Synchronicity, Toronto, Inner City Books, 1980

—, Psyche and Matter, Boston and London, Shambhala Publications, 1992

Waite, A.E., The Pictorial Key to the Tarot, 2nd ed., London, Rider & Co., 1971